About Grace

An Intimate Notebook

Jeannie Sakol and
Caroline Latham

CB

CONTEMPORARY
BOOKS

CHICAGO

Library of Congress Cataloging-in-Publication Data

Sakol, Jeannie.
   About Grace : an intimate notebook / Jeannie Sakol and
Caroline Latham.
      p. cm.
   Includes index.
   ISBN 0-8092-3893-4 :
   1. Grace, Princess of Monaco, 1929–1982. 2. Motion picture
actors and actresses—United States—Biography. 3. Monaco—
Princes and princesses—Biography. I. Latham,
Caroline. II. Title.
DC943.G7S35 1993
944.9'49—dc20   92-37704
[B]   CIP

Published by Contemporary Books, Inc.
180 North Michigan Avenue, Chicago, Illinois 60601
Manufactured in the United States of America
International Standard Book Number: 0-8092-3893-4

About Grace

INTRODUCTION

For those of us old enough to go to the movies then, Grace Kelly *was* the fifties. Her screen persona embodied for us the values of that era. Grace was a *lady*. She always played the good wife or daughter on film, even in compromising situations. Always the cool, blond beauty, Grace was never out of control, even when she was teasing Cary Grant. She was the attractive yet unapproachable woman our mothers told us we ought to be. And although in real life Grace was second-generation Irish, and accordingly snubbed by Philadelphia society, she looked and acted aristocratic, a quality admired in a time when titles were still sought after.

Grace had been able to achieve almost everything: the covers of *Life*, the Oscar nominations, the salary increasing with each contract she signed, the choice of roles that box-office success permitted. With *High Noon*, Grace had gone from supporting player to star and had never look back. And then she gave it all up to marry a prince. It was the fairy-tale ending we had been raised to desire. In a wedding that was an elaborate production masterminded by Hollywood, she became Princess Grace, surely the only fate appropriate to her perfection.

As Princess Grace, she was the perfect wife to Prince Rainier, giving him the heir he needed and the celebrity that brought prosperity to his country. She went through her ceremonial paces with charm and beauty, and she certainly looked the part of a princess. Her activities were the ones you would expect from a good wife and mother, focusing on needy children, the La Leche League, and dainty floral needlepoint. The great dignity with which she imbued the role of princess cloaked the occasional waywardness of her children and the stage-set atmosphere of the kingdom of Monaco. At the time of her death, she was still the perfect role model for the wife and mother of the 1950s.

In the decade since Grace's death, we have begun to learn that the reality of her life was sometimes at odds with the role she often played. She was involved in a series of romances—mostly disastrous—with costars who were obviously father figures. Off the set, she was far from unapproachable, and her instincts seemed to lead her to men who would ultimately reject her. In her later years, she yearned to return to her career, missing the make-believe of Hollywood. She seemed drawn to old lovers, wanted to be with old friends, looked forward to the times she was able to escape from the confining role she had chosen for life.

But for us, the reality of Grace Kelly's life is insignificant compared to the fifties fantasy she represented. The Grace we love is the luminous screen presence, the distant beauty who was never less than a perfect wife, the fairy-tale princess whose wedding we dreamed about (and for Jeannie, who got to attend, a once-in-a-lifetime event that set a standard of romance never since exceeded). The Grace Kelly we love is still there for us, on the screen, in the wonderful photos, and—we hope—in this book for others who remember.

Jeannie Sakol
Caroline Latham
New York, September 1992

ABOUT GRACE

ALBERT AT ALBERT

At age ten Prince Albert attended the Lycée Albert Premier, the Monte Carlo day school named for his great-great-grandfather. The school was close enough to the palace for the young prince to walk there in time for eight o'clock class. Although his mother admitted she was not an early riser, she made a point of breakfasting with her children at 7:30 before packing them off to school.

ALBERT GOES PUBLIC ON HIS SEXUALITY

"I'm straight and always have been," Prince Albert told *People* magazine in 1992. Fully aware of the whispers that he is bisexual or gay, he revealed, "When our family gets together, we joke about it or throw our hands up in desperation because there's very little we can do."

ALBERT "LINKED"

In the summer of 1991 an act of courtesy turned into a wild romantic rumor. As part of his royal duties Prince Albert had welcomed American TV stars Donna Mills, Danielle Brisebois, and Lydia Cornell to Monte Carlo. The international rumor factory "linked" him to Lydia Cornell, the thirty-four-year-old former star of "Too Close for Comfort."

Was history about to repeat itself with another prince-marries-actress scenario? Both subjects of the rumor denied it, and little more was heard about it.

ALBERT LOVED TO CUDDLE

Prince Albert's affectionate nature was evident in childhood, according to his mother's dear friend Judith Balaban Quine: "A kindness emanated from his three-year-old person which could melt a heart of stone." Recalling him as a little boy, she remembered his pure, shy smile and warm, curious eyes, adding, "And Albert loved to cuddle!"

ALBERT'S EDUCATION

After kindergarten at the palace, Prince Albert attended the local Monaco school named for his great grandfather, Prince Albert I, before heading off in 1976 for Cambridge University in England, where he studied English literature. In 1977 he transferred to Amherst College in Massachusetts for a four-year course in political science and economics. At the end of 1981 he signed on as an ensign in the French Navy and served aboard the *Jeanne d'Arc.*

ALWAYS AFRAID OF DRIVING

Grace Kelly was always afraid of driving a car. The reason may have been her poor vision. In her early days in Hollywood, where the automobile is the only way to get around, she rented rather than owned a car and longed for the day when she could have a chauffeur so she would never have to drive herself.

After her marriage she was intimidated by the tortuous curves of the mountain roads surrounding Monaco and drove as little as possible. Even so, on one of her infrequent jaunts behind the wheel she was involved in a minor accident. She felt safest and most comfortable in her old brown Rover 3500, a car she had for years. It was the one she drove to her death one fateful September morning in 1982.

THE AMERICAN APHRODITE (L'APHRODITE AMERICAINE)

French President Charles de Gaulle's appreciative description of Princess Grace, "the American Aphrodite," was expressed during Grace and Rainier's first state visit to Paris in October 1959.

Grace Kelly publicity still from MGM in 1954.

AMERICA'S BICENTENNIAL CELEBRATION

Grace, Rainier, and all three children journeyed to New York in 1976 for the two hundredth anniversary of American independence. They were among those who attended the international gathering of Tall Ships in New York harbor.

ANDREA'S VIOLIN DEBUT

Princess Caroline's eldest child, Andrea, made his violin debut at age seven at a music class recital held at the Princess Grace Theater. As part of a string ensemble, his selections included "The Worm" and "Lazy Song." In addition to his mother, his Aunt Stephanie was also in the audience.

THE ANONYMOUS COVER GIRL

Between 1950 and 1952, Grace Kelly the photographer's model appeared on the covers of such magazines as *Redbook, True Story, True Romance,* and the pre–Helen Gurley Brown *Cosmopolitan.* Just "another pretty face," she appeared unnamed, a situation that changed abruptly with her film success. By 1954 she had appeared on the cover of *Life* magazine, her name in bold type.

ANOTHER APRIL BRIDE

America's onetime White House "princess," President Harry Truman's only child, Margaret, married *New York Times* editor E. Clifton Daniel, Jr., at the Truman family home in Independence, Missouri, just a few days after Grace and Rainier tied the knot in Monaco.

APRICOT-YELLOW NURSERY

When Grace and Rainier's children were small, their quarters at the palace were brightly decorated in apricot yellow with cupboards built by a local carpenter in the shape of dollhouses.

AQUAMARINE KITCHEN

One of Princess Grace's favorite colors was aquamarine. In 1958 when she modernized the family's farmhouse, Roc Agel, she installed an entirely new kitchen with all the latest equipment. The predominant color was aquamarine.

"AREN'T YOU SHOCKED, MISS KELLY?"

On the set of *Dial M for Murder*, director Alfred Hitchcock tried to shatter Grace Kelly's composure by telling off-color stories. "Aren't you shocked, Miss Kelly?" he asked.

Years later Grace remembered answering, "No, I went to a girls' convent school, Mr. Hitchcock. I heard all those things when I was thirteen."

ARI THINKS SHE'S CARY'S SECRETARY

One afternoon in the spring of 1955, shipping tycoon Aristotle Onassis invited his old friend Cary Grant to lunch aboard his yacht, the *Christina*. Ari was still married to his first wife, Tina, for whom the yacht was named. Cary was in the south of France filming *To Catch a Thief*. When he showed up for lunch, Ari thought the prim-looking bespectacled young woman with him was his secretary. Tina, of course, recognized Grace Kelly and smoothed things over. Not being a moviegoer, Ari shrugged charmingly and left the visitors with his wife while he turned his attention to some international business matters.

JEAN-PIERRE AUMONT AND THE SCANDALOUS PHOTOS

What in the 1990s would be seen as playful expressions of affection was jumped on by the international press in 1955 as the makings of a scandal. Despite the fact that neither Grace Kelly nor Jean-Pierre Aumont was married, photographs of them having an intimate lunch at a hideaway restaurant during the Cannes Film Festival caused an uproar of speculation.

A photographer with a telephoto lens had been tipped off—some say by Aumont himself—that the two would be secretly lunching at the Château de la Galère. They were caught kissing and caressing each other across the lunch table. In one shot Grace is holding Aumont's hand, nibbling his fingers.

Pretty tame stuff by later standards, but steamy enough to run in *Paris Match*, *Life*, and other periodicals worldwide.

Oleg Cassini, jealous and incensed, got his brother Igor, the syndicated columnist known as Cholly Knickerbocker, to accuse Aumont of trying to boost his sagging career. When another columnist, Elsa Maxwell, announced that an engagement was imminent and others suggested the couple had secretly married, Prince Rainier, who had just met Grace, thought the game was over before it had begun.

While Grace said she was "embarrassed" by the photographs, and Pierre (as she preferred to call him) said he was also upset, the uproar did not stop them from slipping away to Paris and adjoining suites at the Raphael Hotel. Clearly enjoying themselves in the City of Love, they took long walks, shopped at street stalls, and managed to elude the ever-present paparazzi by escaping to the French countryside for a quiet weekend at Aumont's country house at Rueil-Malmaison with his nine-year-old daughter, Maria-Christina, and relatives of his late wife, Maria Montez. A photograph shows Grace wearing her glasses and knitting placidly in the bosom of Pierre's family.

A few days later, Grace flew back to New York alone amid new rumors of a marriage. A few additional days elapsed before Grace issued a formal statement: "We are just good friends."

Six months later Aumont suffered a broken rib in a minor automobile accident, which led gossip columnist Louella Parsons to announce he had tried to kill himself because of a broken heart!

Grace and Jean-Pierre Aumont's appearance together at the 1955 Cannes Film Festival started tongues wagging and rumors flying all over the world. (UPI/Bettmann)

As a courtesy Grace sent Aumont a telegram about her engagement to Prince Rainier before the formal announcement. On March 27, 1956, three weeks before Grace's wedding, Aumont married Italian actress Pier Angeli's twin sister, Marisa Pavan.

Brief Bio: Born Jean-Pierre Salomons on January 5, 1909, in Paris, he was the son of a wealthy department store merchant and a former actress. At sixteen he enrolled in the Paris Conservatory and made his stage debut in 1930 and his first film appearance in 1931. Quickly becoming an important stage and screen star in France, he interrupted his career during World War II, when he fought with the Free French in Tunisia, Italy, and France and won both the Legion of Honor and the Croix de Guerre. In his first American film, MGM cast him in the lead in a story about the French Resistance, *Assignment in Brittany*. Other American films included *Hilda Crane* with Jean Simmons and *The Devil at 4 O'Clock* with Spencer Tracy and Frank Sinatra.

His first wife was French actress Blanche Montel; his second was actress Maria Montez, whose accidental death left him a widower. He later married, divorced, and then remarried Marisa Pavan. His daughter by Maria Montez is the actress Tina (Maria-Christina) Montez. His brother is noted French film director François Villiers. He was once briefly engaged to actress Hedy Lamarr.

"BA"

Grace Kelly's affectionate name for Clark Gable during the filming of *Mogambo* in Africa, *Ba* means father in Swahili.

BABY GIFTS

Princess Grace's first pregnancy attracted international attention. Thousands of baby gifts arrived at the palace in Monaco. It was a reflection of the time that almost all were intended for a male child. Only one tiny dress appeared among the piles of baby-boy outfits, sweaters, and the like.

The birth of Princess Caroline assured the continuity of the Grimaldis as rulers of Monaco, but there had never been a reigning princess at the head of the tiny state. The way the succession works in Monaco, Princess Caroline was heiress presumptive unless and until a male child, who would then take precedence, was born.

The birth of Prince Albert fourteen months later achieved just that. He became heir to his father, Prince Rainier, and made the citizens of Monaco happy that a prince would continue to rule in the future.

There is no record of what happened to the tiny baby dress!

BALLET SCHOOL RENAMED FOR PRINCESS GRACE

Monaco's Ecole de Danse Classique was founded by Marika Besabrasova in the 1950s. It had fallen on hard times by the time Princess Grace created the Princess Grace Foundation in 1964 as a means of supporting local arts. By renaming the school the Académie de Danse Classique Princesse Grace, she aimed to restore Monte Carlo as the leading European ballet center it had been in the 1920s.

THE BARBIZON NO LONGER "FOR WOMEN ONLY"

As times changed and young women no longer wanted to stay at a "for women only" hotel, New York's celebrated Barbizon

Hotel for Women bowed to the inevitable in 1981, shortening its name to the Barbizon and welcoming men and families. Many of its public rooms, including the huge old-fashioned lobby, are elegant reminders of the hostelry that was home to young actresses such as Grace Kelly and writers such as Sylvia Plath in the 1940s and 1950s. As its brochure points out, the Barbizon is still within walking distance of Bloomingdale's and convenient to museums.

For information, write: The Barbizon, 140 East Sixty-Third Street, New York, NY 10021 (phone: 212/938-5700; fax: 212/753-0360).

BRIGITTE BARDOT ON GRACE

French sexpot Brigitte Bardot scornfully called Princess Grace "L'Altesse Frigidaire"—Her Highness the Icebox.

DR. CHRISTIAAN BARNARD

When the famous South African heart surgeon Dr. Christiaan Barnard visited Monte Carlo in 1968, he was a guest at the Red Cross Ball and danced several times with Princess Grace.

BASHING THE BRIDESMAID

According to a scornful Princess Stephanie interviewed in *Details* magazine in 1991, Judith Balaban Quine's bestselling 1989 memoir, *The Bridesmaids: Grace Kelly and Six Intimate Friends*, is "trash" and rife with stories that aren't true. One example Stephanie cited as being false was about the time Judith's daughter and Princess Caroline flushed Stephanie's head in the toilet and Grace laughed about it.

BASICALLY SHY

In 1968 Princess Grace confessed candidly to *New York Times* correspondent Mark Shivas, "I'm basically a shy person. I don't like being with people I don't know. I had to get over that. It wasn't easy, but when you're thrown suddenly into a life like mine, you just do."

CECIL BEATON ON GRACE

British photographer Cecil Beaton waxed lyrical about Grace Kelly's beauty after a photo session at her Hollywood apartment in 1954: "Grace Kelly belongs to springtime. Pale primrose yellow, with her flaxen hair and dewy complexion, she evokes images of cowslips and curds and whey. Her eyes have a luminous aquamarine beauty. They convey her sense of humor while having the wistfulness of a child."

An early MGM publicity glossy of Grace Kelly circa 1953.

PAUL BELMONDO

The son of French actor Jean-Paul Belmondo, known to American audiences for his 1959 Bogart-style role opposite Jean Seberg in *Breathless*, Paul Belmondo was Princess Stephanie's boyfriend in 1983. She was eighteen, and he was nineteen. Their romance ran its course and settled into an ongoing friendship.

INGRID BERGMAN'S ASHES

Ingrid Bergman died of cancer in August 1982, two weeks before Princess Grace's fatal accident. Shared grief drew Ingrid's son Robertino Rossellini and Grace's daughter Caroline close together. Despite the fact that the two had been friends since childhood, observers misinterpreted their increased time together as a preamble to marriage.

In June 1983 Caroline accompanied Robertino to Danholmen, a tiny island off the southwest coast of Sweden, where Ingrid Bergman had spent the last summers of her life. In accordance with her wishes, her ashes were cast on the Swedish waters. Caroline and Robertino had picked armloads of wild flowers for the ceremony. Together they tossed them in the wake of the boat as a lone saxophonist played an eerie lament.

Rossellini has remained a devoted friend to Princess Caroline through the years of her marriage to Stefano Casiraghi, the birth of their three children, his death, and her subsequent relationship with actor Vincent Lindon.

BERLIOZ THE PARROT

One of Princess Grace's pets at the family hideaway farm at Roc Agel was Berlioz the parrot. She discovered that the colorful bird liked hearing her play the piano.

BESOIN (NEED)

Princess Stephanie's first LP was produced in Europe in 1986. Entitled *Besoin* (*Need*), it sold five million copies, topping the charts with the single "Ouragan" ("Hurricane"). Stephanie's lyrics were all in French.

Baby Grace already knows how to pose for the camera. (Globe Photos)

BIRTH DATES

Princess Grace ....November 12, 1929
Prince Rainier ....May 31, 1923
Princess Caroline ....January 23, 1957
Prince Albert ....March 14, 1958
Princess Stephanie ....February 1, 1965
Andrea Casiraghi ....June 8, 1984
Charlotte Casiraghi ....August 3, 1986
Pierre Casiraghi ....September 5, 1987

BLACK BEACHWEAR

The official six-month mourning period for Stefano Casiraghi ended in December 1991. But when his grieving widow, Princess Caroline, joined her family for a vacation in Jamaica, she continued to wear black even on the beach.

PHYLLIS BLUM, SECRETARY AND FRIEND

Princess Grace's personal secretary and confidante for more than a decade was Phyllis Blum, an American whom she first met in New York in 1956. Blum's initial responsibility was to help the princess pack up her Fifth Avenue apartment. They got on so well, Phyllis moved to Monaco to be her personal secretary. In 1962 she left her job in order to marry Julian Earl, Somerset Maugham's nephew. The two women remained close friends and Grace would sometimes stay at her former secretary's London house during non-official visits to Britain.

JAMES BOND'S SON

Jeffrey Moore, the son of James Bond portrayer Roger Moore, was rumored to be Princess Stephanie's "serious" romance in 1991 despite her assertion that he was only "a pal."

"THE BOSS"

That's what Grace and her siblings called their mother. Rules were strict. The house had to be kept tidy. The four children were not allowed to put their elbows on the table, nor could they leave any food on their plates. A stern disciplinarian, "if they were naughty," Margaret Majer Kelly would use a hairbrush or the back of her hand if a hairbrush was not within reach.

BREAST-FEEDING PRINCESS

The time was the prudish mid-1950s. Bodily functions, especially women's bodily functions, were treated as embarrassments. Among educated and "intellectual" middle-class Americans, breast-feeding was considered primitive in the extreme. A woman who breast-fed her infant in public could be arrested. Bottles, formulas, and rubber nipples replaced natural feeding from the mother's breast.

To Princess Grace, nothing was more essential than the physical and spiritual oneness of a mother breast-feeding her child. She announced her convictions in a newspaper interview and was surprised when many women expressed their disapproval.

It would be a few years before she became involved in the La Leche League, which crusades for breast-feeding. As a first-time mother she followed her conviction that it was normal and right. "I never considered anything else," she said later.

THE BRIDE-TO-BE'S FIRST BOUQUET

Upon stepping on Monacan soil following her arrival in her future domain, Grace Kelly was presented with a bouquet of lilies of the valley by a pair of local children in traditional dress.

BRIDEGROOM FINERY

Prince Rainier himself designed the uniform he wore for the religious ceremony that united him with Grace Kelly. Inspired by nineteenth-century uniforms of Napoléon Bonaparte's marshals, the jacket was black with gold oak leaves on the lapels, gold epaulets on the shoulders, and a dazzle of medals celebrating high points in the Grimaldi family's long and complicated history. The trousers were blue with a gold stripe down the sides. Diagonally across his chest from shoulder to waist hung the red and white sash of the Order of St. Charles, Monaco's highest order.

THE BRIDESMAIDS IN YELLOW

Grace Kelly's six bridesmaids wore custom-made dresses of soft yellow organdy. As described by one of them, Judith Balaban

Quine, in her evocative 1989 memoir, *The Bridesmaids*, "Their small pointed collars led down to slightly dropped shoulders. Our sleeves ballooned out fully to just below our elbows, where they were held in tightly by elasticized cuffs. The bodices of our dresses were strapless, covered only by one layer of sheer organdy, with tiny organdy-covered buttons running down to meet our pleated wide cummerbund waistbands. Our skirts had large enough gathers at each side to assure that, supported by underlayers of stiffer petticoats, they would billow as we walked. Wearing wrist-length white kid gloves, we carried nosegays of three dozen tight yellow rosebuds on lace circles that trailed their yellow satin ribbons down the fronts of our skirts. Small pearl or pearl and diamond earrings were our only jewelry. Our wide-brimmed yellow organdy, custom-made hats had been stiffened lightly with buckram so the brims stood out wide on the tops and sides of our heads."

THE BROOKLYN GRIMALDIS HAVE A BALL!

On the day in June 1978 that Princess Caroline married Philippe Junot in Monaco, Ralph Grimaldi of Brooklyn, New York, invited "everyone named Grimaldi" to a free dinner at his restaurant to celebrate. Instead of the twenty or thirty Grimaldis he expected, more than eighty showed up, and twenty were given a rain check because his restaurant seated only sixty.

Among the honored guests were Thomas Grimaldi of the Canarsie section of Brooklyn, Ray Grimaldi of the Bronx, and Louis Grimaldi, who believed he might actually be related to Prince Rainier because his grandfather had emigrated to America from the Mediterranean coast in the Monaco area.

Host Ralph Grimaldi spared no expense, serving wines, cordials, and desserts with the veal cutlets for which he was locally famous. His newly acquired family of New York Grimaldis toasted the royal Grimaldi bride thousands of miles away. All promised to return to Ralph's restaurant for another Grimaldi reunion.

"Next time they'll pay their own tab," their host warned.

A BROWN ROVER 3500 SALOON

Princess Grace and her daughter Princess Stephanie were returning to Monte Carlo in her brown Rover 3500 Saloon when it plunged off the dangerous mountain road, fatally injuring Grace.

The site of Princess Grace's fatal car crash on September 13, 1982. (Rex Features London)

NANCY BRUBAKER

The name of Grace Kelly's character in *The Bridges at Toko-Ri* was Nancy Brubaker, the wife of navy lieutenant Harry Brubaker, played by William Holden. Based on a novel by James Michener, the film is primarily about men and war, with Holden as a retired World War II pilot called back to duty during the Korean War. In the midst of battle scenes and the life-and-death decisions being made by Holden's superiors,

Grace Kelly publicity still from MGM circa 1954.

Grace Kelly's devoted wife more than held her own in her few critical scenes with Holden. She made audiences feel her resolve to spend as much quality time as possible with her husband on leave in Japan and to exemplify the strong family ties he was being called on to sacrifice, perhaps permanently.

That Grace Kelly and William Holden were in love during the making of *The Bridges at Toko-Ri* may explain the evident chemistry between them. Yet in tribute to her growing talent as an actress, it should be pointed out that her Nancy Brubaker conveyed the subtle ardor of a devoted wife and mother who is worried sick that something terrible will happen to her husband rather than the sudden excitement of a hot new love affair.

ART BUCHWALD AT GRACE'S WEDDING

Columnist Art Buchwald brought his special brand of humor to his coverage of Grace's wedding. Reports of jewel thieves prompted this witty flight of fancy in his syndicated column dated April 17, 1956.

"Prince Rainier is so furious over the jewel robberies that have taken place in Monaco during the last week that he has decided to ban all jewel thieves from the wedding. This drastic measure has raised a howl of protests from jewel robbers of every nationality who were sent there to cover the wedding.

"A topflight jewel thief, who asked that his name not be mentioned, told us in the lobby of the Hotel de Paris, 'I am shocked at the Prince's attitude. We have only stolen jewels from Philadelphia people and we haven't even bothered the Aga Khan. The right of jewel thieves to operate on the Riviera is older than the Magna Carta, and Prince Rainier has no right to bar us from the wedding.' "

WILLIAM F. BUCKLEY'S ANALYSIS

Commenting on Grace Kelly's commitment to her life as wife, mother, princess, and Catholic, William F. Buckley told biographer Steven Englund, "If she had decided to become a nun rather than a princess, there would not have been a distinctive difference in her approach to her vocation." Publisher, author, and host of one of public television's longest-running talk shows, Buckley gives special weight to his analysis because of his own outspoken Catholicism.

"BUMPED OFF" IN THE NAME OF LOVE

To accommodate Grace Kelly's wedding party on the April 4, 1956, Atlantic crossing of the USS *Constitution*, sixty-six travelers who had booked space were "bumped" off that voyage and rescheduled on other ships. To soften the blow, the American Export Line upgraded their accommodations and offered additional courtesies.

ANTHONY BURGESS AND THE JAMES JOYCE FESTIVAL

The celebrated British writer best known for *A Clockwork Orange*, Anthony Burgess lived in Monaco and became a close friend of Princess Grace's. She shared with him her collection of Irish music and the five-hundred-volume library of Irish literature she had amassed over many years. Since Burgess was celebrated in literary circles for his critical works on Irish writer James Joyce, Grace allowed him access to her rare second edition of Joyce's *Ulysses*.

In April 1982 she and Burgess joined forces to create the first Monte Carlo James Joyce Festival. The plan was to attract visitors interested in literature. Their hope to make the festival an annual event was tragically cut short by Grace's fatal accident five months later.

CALL HER "GRACIE"

Grace Kelly's friends and family called her "Gracie." In her letters and signed photographs, "Gracie" is what she called herself. Even as Princess Grace, she and her nearest and dearest referred to her as "Gracie Grimaldi."

MARIA CALLAS'S FUNERAL

On September 16, 1977, opera singer Maria Callas died alone in Paris at age fifty-three, her health failing, her emotions never fully recovered following the death of Aristotle Onassis. Princess Grace and her two daughters were among the many friends and admirers who attended Callas's funeral at the Greek Orthodox Church on rue Georges Bizet on September 20. The solemnity of the occasion was shattered by the obstreperous behavior of photographers trying to get close-up shots of Princess Grace as well as other celebrities.

CAROLINE AT THE CONVENT

In the fall of 1971 fourteen-year-old Princess Caroline was enrolled in St. Mary's Convent School at Ascot, England. To make a good impression on headmistress Sister Bridget, Princess Grace dressed conservatively in a severely tailored suit, pulled her hair back in a bun, and wore her glasses.

Caroline stayed at St. Mary's for two years, graduating in 1973 at age sixteen. Her devotion to her studies and her "serious" approach to life made her subsequent rebellion all the more distressing to her mother, who had naively believed their mother-daughter relationship to be extremely close and mutually trusting.

CAROLINE IS BORN

At 9:27 A.M. on January 23, 1957, Princess Grace gave birth without anesthesia to an eight-pound, three-ounce daughter. Dr. Emile Hervet, the royal obstetrician, described the baby's wails as "like a melody resounding through the palace."

Princess Grace wept.

Prince Rainier kissed his wife, telephoned his mother, and went to the chapel to pray before announcing to his subjects on Radio Monte Carlo, "My beloved wife, the princess, has given birth to a baby princess who has been given the name of Caroline Louise Marguerite. Thank God and rejoice."

Outside the palace a waiting cyclist got the news and raced to the harbor, where a waterfront cannon roared twenty-one times to announce the birth of a girl child. Church bells pealed. Boats in the harbor sounded their horns, including Aristotle Onassis's yacht *Christina*, whose siren could be heard for miles.

In another throwback to earlier times, government officials were brought to the palace to see the infant and be assured that a "true heir" had been born.

The joyful father declared a national holiday. School was dismissed. Monte Carlo's sole prisoner was released from custody. Gambling stopped for the day. Champagne was served throughout the principality. Red-and-white bunting was draped over everything that didn't move.

CAROLINE IS BORN: GRANDPA KELLY COMMENTS

When word of Princess Grace's first child hit her hometown of Philadelphia, a reporter asked her father for his reaction. "Oh, shucks," he said at the news of baby Caroline's arrival, "I wanted a boy!"

CAROLINE MARRIES PHILIPPE

In June 1978 Princess Caroline, twenty-one, married Parisian financier Philippe Junot, thirty-eight, despite her parents' misgivings. There were two separate ceremonies, one civil, the other religious. The thirty-minute civil ceremony was conducted by Louis Roman, president of the Monaco State Council, in the throne room of the palace on June 28. After spending their first wedding night apart, the couple was married again the following day in a nuptial Mass celebrated by the French bishop of Fréjus and Toulon, who had officiated at the wedding of Caroline's parents twenty-two years earlier.

The religious ceremony took place in the small chapel of the palace with only a hundred guests, in quiet contrast to the cathedral wedding of Grace and Rainier attended by more than two thousand.

Caroline's cousin, Grace LeVine, daughter of Princess Grace's sister Lizanne, flew to Monaco from Philadelphia to serve as witness, her blond Kelly beauty in contrast to Caroline's dark, exotic looks.

To prevent intrusion by the paparazzi, two helicopters of the newly created Royal Monaco Air Force circled above the palace.

Grace and Rainier objected to the marriage for three reasons: Junot was seventeen years older than Caroline. He was infamous as an international playboy. The Grimaldi family hoped Caroline would marry one of Europe's more eligible princes, perhaps even Prince Charles of Great Britain.

CAROLINE TO MOVE TO PENNSYLVANIA?

Shortly after Christmas 1991, there were rumors that Princess Caroline and her three children would be moving to Pennsylvania, the home state of her late mother. According to press reports from Monaco, the widowed princess wanted to explore Grace Kelly's roots with her children and send them to American schools. After all, Andrea, Charlotte, and Pierre are one-quarter American.

CAROLINE'S CHRISTENING

On March 4, 1957, Princess Caroline Louise Marguerite was christened in Monaco's St. Nicholas Cathedral in a ceremony conducted by four bishops and fifteen priests. The cathedral was decked with ten thousand branches of white lilacs and tulips. Her godparents were her mother's niece, Margaret David, and her father's second cousin, Prince George Festetics. Her christening gown, trimmed with Valenciennes lace, was a Grimaldi family heirloom that had been worn by both Prince Rainier and his sister Antoinette when they were christened in 1923 and 1921 respectively.

During the ceremonies, Gilles Barthe, bishop of Monaco, touched the baby's ear with his right thumb, intoning, "Be opened so that you may perceive the fragrance of God's sweetness. But you, O devil, depart." Following the services, the proud parents appeared on the palace balcony to show the new princess to the crowd gathered in the square below while flocks of pigeons were released.

CAROLINE'S EARLY CONQUESTS

By the age of eighteen, Princess Caroline had become a striking beauty with a voluptuous figure and a dazzling personality. Having finished school in Britain, she became the rage of Paris, breaking hearts left and right, including those of Henri Giscard d'Estaing, the French president's son, French pop star Philippe Lavil, British jet-setter Nigel Pollitzer, and soon after, the man nearly twice her age whom she would marry and divorce, Philippe Junot.

CAROLINE'S OPERATION

In November 1991, Princess Caroline underwent a gynecological operation to remove a cyst. It required an overnight stay at the Princess Grace Hospital in Monaco, where her mother had died in 1982.

CAROLINE'S SIBLING JEALOUSY

As in any family where a happy-go-lucky toddler is suddenly upstaged by the arrival of a new baby, Princess Caroline at fourteen months was devastated by understandable jealousy when her brother was born. Caroline told *Life* magazine, "I was taken to see my mother. She was holding Albert in her arms. I had a little bouquet of flowers I was supposed to give her, and everyone kept saying, 'Go on, give your mother the flowers,' but I wouldn't. Finally, I just threw them at her."

CAROLINE'S THIRD BIRTHDAY

Already precocious and poised at age three, Princess Caroline played hostess in January 1960 to twenty-five children invited to her birthday party at the palace. She wore an organdy dress with a border motif of orange slices and a paper party hat.

CAROLINE'S THIRD-GRADE CURRICULUM

At the age of eight, Princess Caroline was in the third grade. Her studies included French, German, arithmetic, history, science, geography, sewing, singing, drawing, and catechism. In a class of twenty children, she ranked second.

CAROSTEFAL

The *Carostefal* was the fifty-four-foot Italian cabin cruiser that Prince Rainier bought in 1965. Its name combines the names of the three royal children, Caroline, Stephanie, and Albert. Equipped with air compressors, scuba-diving gear, spears, and fishing tackle, its cruising speed was a jaunty twenty-two knots, making it ideal for quick trips to Sardinia, one of Rainier's favorite destinations.

CARY AND BARBARA HONEYMOON AT THE GRIMALDI PALACE

Following their April 15, 1981, wedding, Cary Grant and Barbara Harris spent their honeymoon in Monaco as guests of the Grimaldis and attended the gala celebration of Grace and Rainier's twenty-fifth wedding anniversary. Another old friend from Hollywood, Frank Sinatra, was also there, serving as master of ceremonies.

JOHN CASSAVETES ON GRACE

Actor/producer John Cassavetes was Grace Kelly's classmate in 1949 at the American Academy of Dramatic Arts. In 1983, a year after her death, he recalled thinking when she graduated, "Isn't it a shame she's too shy ever to amount to anything?"

CASSINI DEFENDS THEIR LOVE

Following Grace's death, Oleg Cassini agreed to be interviewed by "CBS Morning News" correspondent Pat Collins. "Tell us about your *alleged love affair* with Grace Kelly," Collins demanded. Stung by the mean-spirited insinuation, Cassini replied, "We were in love. We were engaged to be married. That is the truth. No more, no less."

CHAMPAGNE AND CAVIAR

Beginning in her earliest days in Hollywood, Grace's favorite snack was champagne and caviar.

CHAPELLE DE LA PAIX

Princess Caroline's second husband, Stefano Casiraghi, is interred in the Chapelle de la Paix (the Chapel of Peace), a private sanctuary on Monte Carlo's avenue des Pins. He died October 3, 1990, in a powerboat accident.

CHARADES

One of Grace Kelly's favorite party games in the 1950s was charades. She and the wedding party played it nightly on the eight-day voyage aboard the USS *Constitution* taking them to Monaco. As Princess Grace she later taught the game to her husband, who became extremely adept and competitive at it.

CHATEAU DE MARCHAIS

Rainier's family estate is at the foot of the Ardennes, located near Paris. About six times the size of Monaco, the property includes a pair of working farms and a herd of Manchurian camels that roam free in the pastures with the cows. Grace, Rainier, and the children spent weekends there during their sojourns in Paris.

A CHERISHED PORTRAIT

Visitors to Monaco's Royal Palace can see the 1974 life-size portrait of Princess Grace painted by Ricardo Macaron and on permanent display in the Mazarin Room.

THE *CHICAGO TRIBUNE* OUTRAGED

The attitude of the *Chicago Tribune* on learning of Grace's engagement to Rainier was one of good-natured outrage. "He's Not Good Enough for a Kelly," the headline ran. "She's too well bred a girl to marry the silent partner in a gambling parlor."

CHILDHOOD DREAMS

According to her older sister, Peggy, the young Grace Kelly not only wanted to be an actress; she also dreamed of being a ballet dancer, a nurse, or an FBI agent.

CHILDHOOD PETS

When Grace Kelly was a child, two of her favorite family pets were boxers named Wrinkles and Siegfried. Once when Siegfried was sick and had to be rushed to the vet, Grace's friend Dottie Langdon recalled, "Grace bawled like a baby."

THE CHILDREN OF THEATRE STREET

The footage for a documentary tracing the history of the Vaganova Choreographic Institute, better known as the Kirov Ballet School, had been shot in 1976 in Leningrad and was being edited by Hungarian director Robert Dornhelm for American producer Earle Mack when Dornhelm approached Princess Grace to do the narration. Prince Rainier gave his enthusiastic approval. The project was ideal for her. Ballet was dear to her heart. The film allowed her to work with producer Jean Dalrymple, who had auditioned her in New York for the role of Roxanne in *Cyrano de Bergerac* a quarter of a century earlier.

Dornhelm photographed Grace at the Monte Carlo Opera House and informally in a boat in the harbor with the wind blowing through her hair.

The Children of Theatre Street won an Academy Award nomination for best documentary of 1977.

"A CHOCOLATE ECLAIR FILLED WITH RAZOR BLADES"

Grace Kelly's former brother-in-law Gabby Davis (Peggy Kelly's first husband) asked Oleg Cassini what it was like to have dinner with Grace's father. According to biographer Arthur H. Lewis, Cassini's succinct reply was "It was like eating a chocolate éclair filled with razor blades."

CHOOSING THEIR SON'S COLLEGE

Prince Rainier and Princess Grace did what ordinary parents do in helping their son choose a university. During one boiling hot summer, they drove to various American campuses—Williams, Amherst, and Princeton among them—until Albert made his preference known: Amherst.

RANDOLPH CHURCHILL EMBARRASSES HIS FATHER

Sir Winston Churchill's son Randolph may have embarrassed his father many times with his personal and political peccadilloes, but one incident that is still remembered happened during the festivities surrounding the wedding of Grace Kelly and Prince Rainier. A regular visitor to Monte Carlo, he was personally annoyed at the inconvenience of the crowds and the press. Losing his temper, he screamed in petulant exasperation, "I didn't come here to meet vulgar people like the Kellys!"

CLOS SAINT-PIERRE

The name of Princess Caroline's two-story pink villa in the Maritime Alps high above Monte Carlo is Clos Saint-Pierre.

COCO THE PARROT

One of Prince Rainier's favorite pets, Coco the parrot, could whistle the Monacan national anthem.

JEAN COCTEAU'S "COMPLIMENT"

A leading figure in the intellectual life of France, Jean Cocteau was a poet, painter, playwright, actor, and creator of such avant-garde films as *The Blood of a Poet* in 1932 and the classic *Beauty and the Beast* in 1945, which is said to have inspired all subsequent film and theatrical versions of the fairy tale. By 1956, when Prince Rainier announced plans to marry Grace Kelly, Cocteau had reached the peak of his eminence in every aspect of the arts, film in particular. His manifesto on the cinema, *Cocteau on Film*, and his elevation to honorary president of the Cannes Film Festival further enhanced his influence on the cultural life of the Riviera.

As his gift to the royal newlyweds, Cocteau wrote a short story called "Compliment," a tale of love. Each wedding guest received a beautifully printed copy.

"COLD AS ICE, BUT . . ."

Alfred Hitchcock told Peter Bogdanovich, "Outwardly, Grace was as cold as ice, but, boy, underneath—she was an inferno!" Referring to the scene in *To Catch a Thief* in which she suddenly kisses Cary Grant full on the lips, gives him a provocative look, and slams the door in his face, Hitchcock said, "It's as though she'd unzipped Cary's fly."

"COME ON, FATTY"

Princess Caroline met Philippe Junot at the famed Paris disco Regine's in the summer of 1976. Instead of flattering her the way most men did, he playfully teased her for being a few pounds overweight. A friend who was with them the night they met recalled Junot saying "Come on, Fatty" as they left the club together.

A COMPETITIVE DORE SCHARY

At a Hollywood luncheon MGM gave in early 1956 for Grace Kelly and her new fiancé Prince Rainier, studio head Dore Schary could not resist taking a competitive stance with the Monégasque ruler. Exactly how big was Monaco? Schary wanted to know. When the prince explained his principality was five miles square, his luncheon host blurted out, "That's not as big as our back lot!"

HOWELL CONANT

Grace Kelly's old friend and trusted photographer Howell Conant was often given "exclusive" rights for certain events beginning with the wedding of Grace and Rainier and including the wedding of Princess Caroline and Philippe Junot.

A CONFUSION OF "KELLYS," OR "HAS ANYBODY HERE SEEN KELLY?"

On the set of *Mogambo* there were two Kellys, one real and the other "reel." Grace Kelly played Linda Nordley, while Ava Gardner played Honey Bear Kelly.

CONSOLATION PRIZE

Grace Kelly was nominated for best supporting actress for her 1953 role in *Mogambo* but lost to Donna Reed for *From Here to Eternity*. When the *Mogambo* crew heard the news, they gave her a consolation plaque inscribed, "This will hold you until next year's Academy Awards." Sure enough, she won the award for best actress for *The Country Girl*.

CONTACT LENSES

Her nearsightedness caused problems for Princess Grace. She hated being photographed wearing glasses on official occasions. On the other hand, if she didn't wear them she had difficulty seeing! Her one attempt at wearing contact lenses was a disaster. It was in the spring of 1966, when she and Jacqueline Kennedy were among the honored guests at the annual *Feria* in Seville. Nobody is exactly sure what happened, but when Grace put the contact lenses in her eyes they were so painful her eyes throbbed and watered. She had to take them out, redo her makeup, and arrive late and flustered to face the waiting photographers.

While it's possible that she mistakenly put the lenses into the wrong eyes, the experience was such that she abandoned the whole idea of contact lenses.

GARY COOPER

He was the first of Grace Kelly's older married lovers. They first met casually while she was making her first Hollywood film, *Fourteen Hours*. Gary Cooper remembered thinking, "She looked educated and as if she came from a nice family. She was certainly a refreshing change from all these sexballs we'd been seeing so much of." There were no real sparks until she was cast as his prim Quaker wife in *High Noon*. The fifty-one-year-old Cooper was twenty-eight years older than Grace. Producer Stanley Kramer told biographer James Spada that Cooper worried how audiences would react to the age difference. "What's an old goat like me doing playing opposite such a young girl?"

Watching Grace in *High Noon*, it's hard to believe that this ethereal creature could be the cause of so much anxiety, jealousy, and potentially dangerous scandal. Cooper had at that time separated from his wife, Rocky, and ended a tempestuous love affair with actress Patricia Neal. The combustion between him and Grace was spontaneous and public. When the gossip columns revealed the romance, the Kelly family in Philadelphia sent Grace's sister Lizanne to California to act as chaperone.

High Noon became an artistic and commercial success. It cost half a million dollars to make and grossed eighteen million. Gary Cooper won the Academy Award for best actor. Grace got slightly lost in the shuffle. The reviews, when they mentioned her at all, were mostly brief and kind. She herself was mortified by her performance. Her passion for Gary Cooper in no way blurred her crystal-clear view of herself and her acting abilities.

Comparing her own performance to Gary Cooper's, she said, "With Gary Cooper, everything is so clear. You look into his face, and see everything he is thinking. I looked into my own face and saw nothing. I knew what I was thinking, but it didn't show. For the first time, I suddenly thought, 'Perhaps I'm not going to be a great star, perhaps I'm not any good after all.' "

In this context her determination to become a fine actress took top priority over any lingering desire to continue her relationship with Cooper. More training was what she needed. Back in New York, she resumed her acting lessons and was expecting to devote considerable time to polishing her skills when legendary director John Ford offered her the chance to costar with Clark Gable and Ava Gardner in *Mogambo*. It seemed she may have learned something from working with Gary Cooper after all.

Brief Bio: Frank James Cooper was born May 7, 1901, in Helena, Montana, the son of a state supreme court justice. He went to school in England, studied agriculture at Wesleyan College, and worked as a guide at Yellowstone National Park. He set out for California in the hope of becoming a newspaper cartoonist but was soon playing cowboy "extras" in movie westerns because he was fearless on a horse. Tall, handsome, laconic, he made the transition from silent films to talkies with ease. Film directors like Ernst Lubitsch and Frank Capra brought out his latent talents for comedy and common-man heroics.

Apart from Grace Kelly, the famous women who were enthralled by him included Lupe Velez, Audrey Hepburn, Patricia Neal, and the "It" girl of the 1920s, Clara Bow, who nicknamed him Studs. His romance with Prince Rainier's mistress of many years, Gisele Pascal, in 1955 is said to have marked *fini* to that relationship and left the prince emotionally free to pursue other possibilities for marriage, including the film star Grace Kelly.

Among Gary Cooper's hundred films, the most noteworthy

have been *Mr. Deeds Goes to Town, Sergeant York, For Whom the Bell Tolls, The Fountainhead,* and *High Noon.*

He married only once. His wife was socialite Veronica "Rocky" Balfe, who also appeared in films as Sandra Shaw. Despite his many affairs, they stayed married until his death in 1961.

COSBY'S QUICK QUIP

Bill Cosby has always been known for his quick wit and exquisite timing. An example of this was revealed by Jeffrey Robinson in his biography of Grace and Rainier. When Cosby met Princess Grace, someone suggested, "You probably already know each other because you both come from Philadelphia." To this, Cosby responded, "Yes, of course we know each other. Her family owned my family."

COUSIN JEAN FAINTS

Grace's cousin Jean Goit fainted during her wedding ceremony. As recalled by Judith Balaban Quine, she was quietly taken out of the cathedral, where a hastily summoned doctor brought her around.

JACQUES COUSTEAU'S HOME BASE

For many years famed oceanographer Jacques Cousteau made his headquarters in Monaco at the Oceanographic Institute founded in 1910 by Prince Rainier's great grandfather Prince Albert I.

Known as the "seagoing prince" and the "scientist prince," Albert founded the institute for the study of marine science. His many expeditions took him to foreign parts as diverse as the Azores, North and South America, and the northern shores of Norway. He also endowed foundations for the study of paleontology and anthropology.

In Monaco today the Oceanographic Institute is a museum

of marine sciences and an aquarium. Built in the ornate and grandiose style of the turn of the century, its massive rooms display Prince Albert's collections of marine fauna, specimens of sea creatures, models of his laboratory ships, and crafts made from products of the sea.

Below ground is the aquarium, where rare species of multicolored fish from all the seas of the world swim in ninety tanks supplied with water directly from the Mediterranean. In a separate three-hundred-seat theater, Jacques Cousteau's films about his explorations and adventures are shown on a regular schedule.

Clearly Prince Rainier inherited his passion for the sea from his ancestor. He has often been quoted as saying if he had not been born a prince, he'd have become a sailor.

"A CRAZED NYMPHOMANIAC"

Princess Stephanie's description of her own lifestyle during the period after her mother's death was that of "a crazed nymphomaniac." Speaking in defense of her affairs with a race car driver, actor, pool boy, record producer, and others, she told *People* weekly, "People imagine that everything is easy when you're a princess, but we're still human beings."

BING CROSBY

Early in 1952 Hollywood, twenty-three-year-old Grace Kelly was one of several young actresses who dated Bing Crosby. His wife Dixie's lingering battle with cancer ended with her death in November that year, while Grace was in Africa filming *Mogambo*. According to biographer Jane Ellen Wayne, Crosby took advantage of his friendship with his next-door neighbors, Sue and Alan Ladd, by bringing Grace to their house for late-night swimming in their pool. There were some hints of gossip about the affair, but for the most part an adoring public still idolized Crosby and the press continued to portray him as a devoted father and heartbroken widower after Dixie's death.

The romance then petered out until suddenly, in 1954,

Grace was cast as Crosby's wife in *The Country Girl*. After two years of bachelorhood he fell madly in love with his costar and proposed marriage.

In the meantime, Grace was falling in love with her other costar, William Holden, while also keeping Oleg Cassini dangling. Bing Crosby eventually got the message that the answer to his proposal was negative. Some observers insist he carried a torch for Grace for years afterward.

Brief Bio: Harry Lillis Crosby was born May 2, 1904. He was a vocalist and drummer while attending Gonzaga University, sang with Paul Whiteman's band in 1926, and made his film debut in 1930. He appeared in film shorts, performed in nightclubs, and had his own radio show; its theme song was "Where the Blue of the Night." In the 1930s when Grace Kelly was a little girl, his records sold in the millions, making him America's most popular "crooner."

By the 1940s he had teamed with Bob Hope for a series of *Road to . . .* movies and moved on to serious dramatic roles with his Academy Award–winning portrayal of a Catholic priest in *Going My Way*. In addition to *The Country Girl*, he costarred with Grace Kelly in her final feature film, *High Society*, in which ironically their characters marry at the end. Their duet of Cole Porter's "True Love" from the soundtrack surprised everyone by going first gold and then platinum.

One of the entertainment industry's wealthiest men, Crosby amassed a fortune estimated at upward of four hundred million dollars. In 1957 he married actress Kathryn Grant, thirty years his junior, adding three more children to the four sons from his first marriage. He died in 1977 at the age of seventy-three while playing golf.

"A CROSS BETWEEN AIMEE SEMPLE MCPHERSON AND QUEEN ELIZABETH!"

Frank Sinatra's 1956 assessment of his friend and *High Society* costar was "a cross between Aimee Semple McPherson and Queen Elizabeth." Comparing Grace to the volatile evangelist and the no-nonsense British monarch may have sounded sarcastic, but it was said fondly. He also called the future princess of Monaco "the squarest person I ever knew."

CUSTODY FIGHT FOR RAINIER

After their parents were divorced in 1933, Prince Rainier and his sister, Princess Antoinette, were victims of a bitter custody fight between their mother, Princess Charlotte, and their father, Prince Pierre. At one point, Prince Pierre tried to kidnap his ten-year-old son and had to be stopped under the threat of law.

According to biographer Sarah Bradford, the war between mother and father resulted in the children spending most of their time with their grandfather, Prince Louis, until it was decided that Rainier should have an English education. He was sent first to Summerfields, a small preparatory school in St. Leonard's-on-Sea near Hastings, and then to Stowe in Buckinghamshire.

To be a foreigner and Catholic in a Protestant English public school before World War II was, Bradford explains, "a cardinal sin in the eyes of your fellow boys; to be chubby and insecure gave them the ammunition with which to torture you." Example: Prince Rainier was taunted as "fat little Monaco."

After the young prince ran away from school twice and amidst rumors of another kidnapping threat by Prince Pierre, Rainier's grandfather allowed him to leave England and continue his education at the Le Rosey School in Switzerland where he was treated with respect and friendliness.

DANCED FOR HER WEDDING, MARRIED HER SISTER-IN-LAW

As part of the Rainier-Kelly wedding festivities, the London Festival Ballet Company appeared in Monte Carlo in a special performance starring Margot Fonteyn, Belinda Wright, and John Gilpin. Nearly three decades later and after Grace's death, John Gilpin married her sister-in-law, Princess Antoinette.

VIRGINIA DARCY

The flamboyant red-haired MGM studio hairdresser who accompanied Grace Kelly on the eight-day ocean journey from New York to Monte Carlo was Virginia Darcy. For all her exquisite beauty, Grace had "problem" hair, thin, silken, and difficult to control. Since every night at sea demanded the appearance of an elegant bride-to-be, Virginia's job was to make ingenious use of chignons and bunches of pin-on curls to achieve the expected glamour. Judith Balaban Quine describes Virginia as having had a raucous laugh, a big heart, and a warm spirit during the Atlantic voyage and for all the wedding festivities that followed.

THE DEATH OF THE FIRST GRACE KELLY

Princess Grace was named after her father's younger sister, Grace, a beautiful and beloved member of the Kelly family whose life was tragically short. One day in the winter of 1920, she and her older brother Jack went ice-skating on Gostine Lake near their Philadelphia home. After a few hours of vigorous activity, they were about to leave when Jack decided to try out his speed for a few more turns around the pond.

He told Grace to stay behind and take off her skates, but she was as full of spirit as her brother. The overexertion was too much for what turned out to be a weak heart. She suffered a heart attack and died. At her funeral her mother (Princess Grace's grandmother) said, "The sun will never shine quite the same for me again."

This "first" Grace Kelly's ambition was to be a great

actress. A polished mimic, she sang Harry Lauder songs dressed in a kilt and seemed destined for success in vaudeville along with her brother Walter Kelly. She was only twenty at her death.

OLIVIA DE HAVILLAND'S HUSBAND: ACCIDENTAL MATCHMAKER

It was a chance meeting with Olivia De Havilland and her husband that literally started the chain of events that led to Grace Kelly's marriage to Prince Rainier. In May 1955 Grace Kelly had taken the famed Blue Train from Paris to the Riviera for the Cannes Film Festival. Also aboard the overnight train were actress Olivia De Havilland and her French husband, Pierre Galante, the editor of *Paris Match* magazine. It was Pierre's idea to do a cover story on Grace and to have her photographed in Monte Carlo with the young bachelor Prince Rainier, a combination of film royalty and European royalty.

DEN WALL MOTTOES

The walls of Princess Grace's den reflected her American sense of humor. Stuck haphazardly on the wood paneling were such mottoes as "In God we trust. All others pay cash" and "We'd love to help you out, which way did you come in?"

LADY DIANA GETS THE LOWDOWN ON BEING A PRINCESS FROM GRACE

On her first official night out in London after the announcement of her engagement to Prince Charles in March 1981, Lady Diana Spencer attended a gala at Goldsmith Hall for the benefit of the Royal Opera House in Covent Garden. Prince Charles was the patron of the event. Princess Grace appeared on the program in a poetry reading and was introduced to Charles's fiancée.

When Princess Grace met the future princess of Wales, she instantly recognized her shyness and physical discomfort in the famous slinky black strapless gown that caused such a stir. At one point Grace became maternal and comforting to the young woman, who was in the same age bracket as her own children, and led her to the powder room, ordering her to relax. When Diana asked if this was what her life was going to be like, Grace hugged her and said, "It gets worse!"

A genuine caring friendship between the younger and the older princesses began to evolve. Princess Grace attended the royal wedding in July. They stayed in touch and in all likelihood would have become close, but time ran out for Princess Grace the following year. Princess Diana flew to Monaco immediately to show her affection and respect at the funeral.

DID GRACE REALLY BELIEVE SHE WOULD GIVE UP ACTING FOREVER?

No, according to her dear friend and bridesmaid Rita Gam. In the 1987 TV documentary "Grace Kelly: The American Princess," Gam said candidly, "I don't think Grace really believed that she was going to give up acting when she became Princess Grace of Monaco. I think that the reality of that probably struck her somewhere in the middle of the Mediterranean after the honeymoon began."

EMIL DIESTEL

In 1947 Emil Diestel was secretary of the American Academy of Dramatic Arts Board of Trustees in New York City when Grace Kelly applied for admission. Impressed by the fact that she was playwright George Kelly's niece, Diestel gave her a lengthy piece of dialogue from Kelly's play *The Torch Bearers* to memorize overnight.

Although enrollment for the term was closed, Diestel noted Grace's good personality, stage presence, dramatic instincts, and positive imagination. Recommending her for admission, he wrote, "Lovely child. Should develop well."

Grace was admitted. Diestel's words proved to be prophetic.

A DIOR EVENING GOWN AND LOW HEELS

On her first night out with Prince Rainier in New York after their engagement was announced, Grace Kelly wore a gorgeous Christian Dior gown with low heels so she would not look taller than her new fiancé. They attended a gala ball at the Waldorf-Astoria Hotel and danced until 4:00 A.M. at the Harwyn, New York's most sophisticated nightclub of the 1950s.

DISAPPOINTMENT FOR MARGARET KELLY

Traditionally the bride's family arranges the wedding. That's what Margaret Kelly wanted to do for her daughter Grace. For a brief moment after the engagement was announced, her thoughts were filled with plans for the biggest and most splendid wedding Philadelphia—and the world—had ever seen. Her disappointment was acute when Prince Rainier explained that his marriage was a matter of state. Marrying him would make her daughter the reigning princess of Monaco. Therefore the wedding would have to take place in Monaco according to its civil and religious traditions.

DOGS IN THE DINING ROOM

Princess Grace's cousin, Charles V. Kelly, Jr., had a surprise waiting for him the first time he visited the palace at Monaco. As he recalled to Kelly family biographer Arthur H. Lewis, he refused to eat in the dining room unless a pair of dogs was removed. The food for the dogs was prepared in silver bowls that were passed from Rainier to Grace for their approval before being set before the pets in a corner of the room.

Observing the ritual with disgust, cousin Kelly said later, "I told Grace either the dogs go or I go. I had no intention of eating my meal with a pair of slobbering beasts.

"The dogs went. I stayed."

Grace Kelly, dog lover.

"DON'T CALL US; WE'LL CALL YOU!"—THIRTY-EIGHT TIMES

In 1949 the neophyte actress Grace Kelly went on thirty-eight casting calls for Broadway shows and was never called back for so much as a second reading.

"DON'T WORRY, MADONNA . . ."

Princess Stephanie sent that message to superstar Madonna by way of rock journalist Henry Edwards during an interview for *Details* magazine in 1991. When Edwards asked "Should Madonna be worried?" about Stephanie as competition, the princess replied, "There's one Madonna and there's one Stephanie. I won't go to the same designers she does or dye my hair blonde. There's room for everybody."

EARLY ANALYSIS OF GRACE KELLY'S APPEAL

In June 1954 *Look* magazine gave these reasons for Grace Kelly's rapid rise to stardom: "She has a quality of maturity that flatters middle-aged male stars who usually shy away from too-young leading ladies, and an inner warmth and aura of sex that suggests the early Ingrid Bergman."

EASTER WITH THE SINATRAS

In 1973, Grace, Rainier, their three children, and her namesake niece, Grace LeVine, spent Easter week as guests of Frank and Barbara Sinatra at their Palm Springs, California, compound.

PRESIDENT EISENHOWER'S ENVOY SNEERS

President Eisenhower's personal representative at the wedding of Grace Kelly and Prince Rainier was America's leading hotel owner, Conrad Hilton. Seemingly annoyed at having this assignment thrust on him, he lost his diplomatic cool when someone suggested he might want to build a Monte Carlo Hilton Hotel. "We never build in resorts or small towns."

GEORGIE ELGIN

The name of Grace Kelly's character in *The Country Girl* was Georgie Elgin. In a striking contrast to her usually glamorous image, she sacrificed her gossamer blond hair and superbly

Grace Kelly, as the emotionally battered Georgie Elgin in The Country Girl, *resists the advances of William Holden before ultimately capitulating.*

proportioned figure for the drab brown hairdo and unflattering clothes of an emotionally battered wife. The demands of the role were enormous as she endured the abuse of her actor husband, played by Bing Crosby, and stoically accepted stage director William Holden's assumption that she was to blame for Bing's problems. For admirers of Grace's flawless beauty, there were flashbacks of Georgie's happier and prettier days. In one of the angry scenes between her and Holden, Georgie reached into the core of her being—and perhaps every battered woman's being—when she said all she yearned for was a room of her own where she could be alone.

Although Bing Crosby garnered the major share of the reviews for his outstanding performance as the manipulative and thoroughly selfish husband, Grace's Georgie was widely lauded and wound up winning her the 1954 Academy Award for best actress. As a romantic sidebar, Georgie's love scenes with William Holden were as steamy as they seemed. They fell wildly in love and carried on an affair for more than a year.

ELITCH GARDENS

The oldest and most prestigious summer repertory company in America in the early 1950s was Elitch Gardens in Denver, Colorado. Founded in 1890, its theater was situated in a large amusement park owned by the Gurtler family. Grace was offered a modest $125 per week. Her agent, Edith Van Cleve, advised her to take it and be happy that she would have a long summer of acting experience before returning to Hollywood.

The pace was grueling. According to company producer Whitfield Connor, the group was expected to learn and perform in ten plays in eleven weeks. During that summer of 1951, twenty-one-year-old Grace fell in love with actor Gene Lyons, the first "adult" passion of her life.

QUEEN ELIZABETH DECLINES THE INVITATION

Although officially invited to the wedding of Prince Rainier and Grace Kelly, Queen Elizabeth II of Great Britain sent her

Queen Elizabeth II of Britain and Prince Charles. She declined Prince Rainier's invitation to attend his wedding to Grace Kelly in 1956. Eighteen years later, Prince Charles declined to comment on his rumored interest in Princess Caroline as a potential bride. (Photo courtesy of British Information Services.)

regrets—and a gold serving tray as a wedding gift. What was hurtful to Rainier and his new princess was Elizabeth's unmistakable snub. As the ruler of one country, it would have been royal courtesy to attend the wedding of the ruler of another, admittedly smaller, country.

As royalty watchers agreed, if Elizabeth herself found it "inconvenient" to attend, she could have sent her sister, Princess Margaret, or another of her royal relatives. Whether there was another reason for Buckingham Palace's attitude is unknown. The official story portrayed the problem as one of protocol. Since Her Majesty had never met His Serene Highness Prince Rainier, neither she nor any member of the royal family could "properly" attend the ceremony.

"MISS ELLIE" IN GRACE'S FIRST FILM

Barbara Bel Geddes, known to TV audiences for her role as Miss Ellie in "Dallas," also had a small part in Grace Kelly's first film, *Fourteen Hours*. Bel Geddes went on to major roles on Broadway and in films and received an Oscar nomination for best supporting actress for her role in *I Remember Mama*.

EMBARRASSED BY AVA

On location in Africa for *Mogambo* in 1952, Grace Kelly was challenged by the uninhibited behavior of costar Ava Gardner, who swore like a longshoreman and made graphic remarks about then-husband Frank Sinatra's sexual equipment. When Sinatra joined Ava, Grace complained that since their tent was next to hers she became an embarrassed eavesdropper on their high-volume shenanigans.

ERIN GO BLAH

Her Irish Kelly bloodline notwithstanding, Princess Stephanie is persona non grata in Ireland and may never again be able to visit her mother's ancestral land. In early 1992 the multitalented fashion designer, actress, model, and singer agreed to appear in Dublin at a gala benefit for the National Council for the Blind. The council had agreed to fly Stephanie to Dublin first-class and to pay for her hotel and limousine expenses. At the last minute Stephanie sent the council a bill for $100,000. Since the gala was expected to raise only $15,000, the organizers were forced to cancel Stephanie's appearance even though invitations had been sent out. Because of the resulting brickbats in the Irish press, Stephanie then announced she would not go to Dublin— because of bad treatment from the press!

In her stead, rock legend Bill Wyman agreed to appear at the gala for free.

In retrospect, the entire brouhaha might stem from the bad vibrations of the date of the gala—Friday the thirteenth—of March!

AN "ERNEST" DECISION

In March 1956, having completed filming *High Society*, Grace Kelly was anxious to leave Hollywood for New York. Her wedding in Monaco was a month away. She had hundreds of

Grace's last public appearance in Hollywood before marrying Prince Rainier was to present an Oscar to Ernest Borgnine at the 1955 Academy Awards. (UPI/Bettmann)

last-minute preparations to make before sailing on the USS *Constitution*. But there was also the Academy Awards ceremony on March 21. In her final role as a member of the film community, she postponed her departure so as to present the best actor award to Ernest Borgnine for *Marty*.

FATHER COMPLEX

Friends and family who were close to Grace Kelly from childhood commonly refer to the actress's abiding need for her father's approval and affection, which tragically she never got despite her Academy Award–winning success as an actress, her international fame and respect as princess of Monaco, her three children, and her unending "good works" for charity and the arts. This "father complex" explains for many her early obsessive passion for older accomplished men such as Clark Gable, Ray Milland, Gary Cooper, and Bing Crosby, who could give her the love and approval she so desperately sought.

A FATHER'S ADVICE

When Grace Kelly told her parents that she was going to New York to enroll at the American Academy of Dramatic Arts, her father said, "It's a dangerous profession, both before and after you reach the top. If you go into this, you must dedicate yourself to it. You can't be halfway about it. There will be sacrifices, lots of them. While others play, you will have to be getting your rest so that you will look nice the next day. And once you reach the top you become public property. There will be no privacy. The public will make great demands on you. Are you ready to pay the price?"

Neither father nor daughter could know in 1947 how accurate his predictions would be.

Grace assured her father she was willing to pay the price of fame, adding, "I won't disappoint you."

FDR HONORS JACK KELLY

On October 12, 1940, the Democratic party held its Presidential Convention in Philadelphia. President Franklin Delano Roosevelt was the party's unopposed candidate for a third term. The president gave the honor of introducing him at Convention Hall to his friend and supporter John B. Kelly. As eleven-year-old Grace and the rest of the family watched from a special box, her father stepped to the podium, raised his arms to quiet the exuberant crowd, and said, "Ladies and gentlemen, the president of the United States."

FEAR OF DYING

According to Madge Tivey-Faucon, Princess Grace's former lady-in-waiting, in a 1964 interview, Grace had "a terrible fear of dying in an airplane or in a car. . . ." Tivey-Faucon attributed this fear to Grace's Scorpio birth sign, which gave her " a passionate temperament—mysterious, extremely physical, eager to seize all the joys of fortune and love—for life is brief, death is at hand."

A FEMINIST, YES, BUT . . .

Interviewed in 1976 by Curtis Bill Pepper in *McCall's* magazine, Princess Grace said, "I'm very much a feminist at heart. I think women can do whatever they set their minds to do. But I also think that in a man-woman relationship, the man should be the head of the family and unchallenged by a woman.

"It's a partnership in that two people should keep their own identities, not squash the other. But it can't be 50-50 and work. If a woman goes into marriage thinking that, she's in for a big shock because she has to give more than 50 percent to make her marriage successful."

FEZ AND DARK GLASSES

Ex-king Farouk of Egypt was the only near-royal guest at Grace Kelly's wedding. He was instantly recognizable because of his enormous girth, dark glasses, and dark red fez.

FIG LEAVES IN THE POWDER ROOM

When Princess Grace and her two oldest children visited Chicago in 1976, they spent an evening at Zorine's, a private discotheque. The management was concerned about the propriety of the pictures of frontally nude men adorning the walls of the powder room and hastily had them strategically covered with fig leaves before the royal party arrived.

FILMOGRAPHY

FOURTEEN HOURS: (1951): Screenplay by John Paxton from a *New Yorker* article by Joel Sayre, directed by Henry Hathaway, produced by Sol S. Siegel for 20th Century Fox. *Cast:* Paul Douglas, Richard Basehart, Howard da Silva, Barbara Bel Geddes, Agnes Moorehead, Robert Keith, Martin Gabel, Debra Paget, Jeffrey Hunter, Grace Kelly, James Warren, Frank Faylen, Jeff Corey, James Millican, Donald Randolph, George MacQuarrie, George Putnam, Michael Fitzmaurice.

A critically acclaimed drama based on the true story of a mentally disturbed man who stands for fourteen hours on the ledge of a Manhattan hotel window, threatening to jump. Richard Basehart plays the man, Barbara Bel Geddes his girlfriend. Grace Kelly makes her feature film debut in a small scene in a lawyer's office.

HIGH NOON: (1952): Screenplay by Carl Foreman, directed by Fred Zinnemann, produced by Stanley Kramer, a Stanley Kramer Production released by United Artists. *Cast:* Gary Cooper, Thomas Mitchell, Lloyd Bridges, Katy Jurado, Grace Kelly, Otto Kruger, Lon Chaney, Henry Morgan, Ian MacDonald, Eve McVeagh, Harry Shannon, Lee Van Cleef, Bob Wilke, Sheb Woolley, Tom London, Ted Stanhope, Larry Black, William Phillips.

The mythic western about the lawman torn between ethics and a profound desire for a settled life with his new bride. Gary Cooper earned an Academy Award for his portrayal of sheriff Will Kane. Grace Kelly, in her role as his Quaker wife who must choose between nonviolence and her husband's life, makes the most of her few scenes, one in particular with Cooper's discarded mistress, played by Katy Jurado.

MOGAMBO: (1953): Screenplay by John Lee Mahin, based on a play by Wilson Collison, directed by John Ford, produced by Sam Zimbalist for MGM. *Cast:* Clark Gable, Ava Gardner, Grace Kelly, Donald Sinden, Philip Stainton, Eric Pohlmann, Laurence Naismith, Dennis O'Dea.

Grace Kelly plays the inhibited wife of anthropologist Sinden who falls passionately in love with white hunter Gable in this remake of the 1932 Gable scorcher *Red Dust*, shot on location in Africa. Kelly plays the Mary Astor role opposite Ava Gardner, who was nominated for an Academy Award, in the Jean Harlow role.

DIAL M FOR MURDER: (1954): Screenplay by Frederick Knott from his play, produced and directed by Alfred Hitchcock, a Warner Brothers release. *Cast:* Ray Milland, Grace

Robert Cummings as Mark, Grace Kelly's secret lover in Dial M for Murder, *playing a mystery writer who helps save her from execution.*

Kelly, Robert Cummings, John Williams, Anthony Dawson, Leo Britt, Patrick Allen, George Leigh, George Alderson, Robin Hughes.

In Grace Kelly's first Hitchcock film she plays the wife Ray Milland plots to murder for her money. When she kills the hired assassin, Milland twists the evidence so that she is tried, convicted, and sentenced to death. Her affair with crime novelist Cummings and the efforts of police inspector John Williams make for a chilling and happy Hitchcock ending.

REAR WINDOW: (1954): Screenplay by John Michael Hayes from a short story by Cornell Woolrich, produced and directed

Jimmy Stewart leaves his broken leg behind on the set of Rear Window *as he and costar Grace Kelly relax after a long day before the cameras.*

by Alfred Hitchcock for Paramount Pictures. *Cast*: James Stewart, Grace Kelly, Wendell Corey, Thelma Ritter, Raymond Burr, Judith Evelyn, Ross Bagdasarian, Georgine Darcy, Sarah Berner, Frank Cady, Jesslyn Fast, Rand Harper, Irene Winston, Harris Davenport.

Grace really comes into her own as the gorgeous, sexy, sophisticated girlfriend of photographer James Stewart, who is confined to a wheelchair with a broken leg. His preoccupation with the goings-on in apartments across a courtyard is shown in counterpoint to Grace's provocative attempts to seduce him into marriage, her ploys ranging from a mouth-watering negligee to a take-out gourmet dinner from the 21 Club. Suspense accelerates when Stewart sees a murder and Kelly tries to help trap the killer and is herself trapped.

THE COUNTRY GIRL: (1954): Screenplay by George Seaton based on the play by Clifford Odets, directed by Seaton, produced by William Perlberg, a Perlberg-Seaton Production

A moment of high drama in The Country Girl *(left to right): Grace Kelly, Bing Crosby, William Holden.*

released by Paramount Pictures. *Cast*: Bing Crosby, Grace Kelly, William Holden, Anthony Ross, Gene Reynolds, Jacqueline Fontaine.

Grace Kelly gives a breathtaking, Oscar-winning performance as the drab, abused wife of Bing Crosby, the manipulative broken-down alcoholic actor whom William Holden wants to star in a Broadway production. The tug-of-war waged between Kelly and Holden for Crosby ultimately reveals the harrowing truth about the marriage. Grace exchanges her usual glamour for a dreary hairstyle, little makeup, eyeglasses, and a gloomy cardigan. Having repressed her emotions to avoid feeling pain, she resists her sexual longing for William Holden until suddenly it explodes in a wild embrace.

GREEN FIRE: (1954): Screenplay by Ivan Goff and Ben Roberts, directed by Andrew Marton, produced by Armand Deutsch for MGM. *Cast*: Stewart Granger, Grace Kelly, Paul

Coffee plantation owner sips—you guessed it—coffee on location in Colombia for Green Fire.

Grace Kelly on location in the mountains of Colombia, South America, for Green Fire.

Douglas, John Ericson, Murvyn Vye, Jose Torvay, Robert Tafur. The "green" is the emeralds that mining engineer Granger wants to snatch from a South American mountainside. The "fire" is his love scenes with coffee plantation owner Grace Kelly. The story is the kind of banal adventure drama that makes Grace's reluctance to do it understandable.

THE BRIDGES AT TOKO-RI: (1954): Screenplay by Valentine Davies based on the novel by James A. Michener, directed by Mark Robson, produced by William Perlberg and George Seaton, a Perlberg-Seaton Production presented by Paramount Pictures. *Cast*: William Holden, Grace Kelly, Fredric March, Mickey Rooney, Robert Strauss, Charles McGraw, Keiko Awaji, Earl Holliman, Richard Shannon, Willis B. Bouchey.

Grace Kelly's touching role as the wife of navy pilot William Holden illuminates the personal torments of the Korean War. Holden is an ex–World War II pilot who resents being called up again for a dangerous mission in Korea; Kelly is the wife who visits him in Japan, a vivid and passionate reminder of the family life he feels he has earned with his previous bravery.

TO CATCH A THIEF: (1955): Screenplay by John Michael Hayes based on a novel by David Dodge, directed and produced by Alfred Hitchcock for Paramount Pictures. *Cast*: Cary Grant, Grace Kelly, Jessie Royce Landis, John Williams, Charles Vanel, Brigitte Auber.

American heiress Grace Kelly is on the French Riviera to catch a husband. Cary Grant is the retired cat burglar out to catch the jewel thief who has been imitating his style. Grace not only thinks Cary's the "cat's" pajamas; she makes no bones about wanting to get into them. Set against the lush background of Monte Carlo and the environs she would soon be enjoying as Princess Grace of Monaco, the film is almost as much of a fairy-tale romance as her real-life romance with Prince Rainier. Grace is superbly in control as the cool, witty, exquisitely gorgeous, articulate, and sexy American who is both rich enough and astute enough to find the man she wants—and get him!

THE SWAN: (1956): Screenplay by John Dighton based on the play by Ferenc Molnár, directed by Charles Vidor, produced by Dore Schary for MGM. *Cast*: Grace Kelly, Alec Guinness, Louis Jourdan, Agnes Moorehead, Jessie Royce Landis, Brian Aherne, Leo G. Carroll, Estelle Winwood, Van Dyke Parks, Christopher Cook, Robert Coote.

With her name at the top of the credits for the first—and last—time, Grace's role is rife with ironies. She plays a princess (Alexandra by name) who is engaged to marry (more irony) a prince named Albert (a hereditary name in the Grimaldi family and the name of her future son) played by Alec Guinness. Unlike herself, Molnár's princess is born to her position, a shy creature in a totally unreal Ruritanian country. Her betrothal to Guinness has been arranged, although her true love is the handsome music teacher, Louis Jourdan. Seeing the film with the knowledge of what was to come in Grace's life is fascinat-

Princess Alexandra (Grace Kelly) resisting the passionate embrace of the music teacher (Louis Jourdan) in The Swan.

ing, considering the movie's philosophical discussions of royal responsibility and sacrifice.

HIGH SOCIETY: (1956): Screenplay by John Patrick based on the Philip Barry play *The Philadelphia Story,* music and lyrics by Cole Porter, directed by Charles Walters, produced by Sol S. Siegel for MGM. *Cast:* Bing Crosby, Grace Kelly, Frank Sinatra, Celeste Holm, John Lund, Louis Calhern, Sidney Blackmer, Louis Armstrong, Margalo Gilmore, Lydia Reed, Gordon Richards.

In this her last feature film, Grace plays the Tracy Lord role originated by Katharine Hepburn. Interestingly, the diamond engagement ring she wears is the "friendship" ring given to her by Prince Rainier when she accepted his proposal. Also interesting is the fact that Hepburn's earlier costars were Cary Grant and James Stewart, who subsequently became Grace's leading men. In this version Tracy's ex-husband is Bing Crosby and the smitten reporter Frank Sinatra. While critics compared the film itself and Grace in particular unfavorably to the Hepburn original, it was a box office smash as Grace Kelly fans swarmed to the movie house to see Princess Grace in her final film appearance.

THE WEDDING OF THE CENTURY: (1956): A documentary film of the Grace Kelly–Prince Rainier wedding, made by MGM with a Monégasque crew and distributed worldwide. The share of the profits allocated to Grace and Rainier was turned over to the Monaco Red Cross.

THE FINAL TRAGIC PREGNANCY

In 1967, during a visit to Montreal's Exposition, Princess Grace suddenly collapsed and was rushed to the hospital. Doctors discovered that she was pregnant but that the fetus she was carrying had been dead for several days. The tragedy depressed her. She wanted more children. She was only thirty-eight and presumably could become a mother again. But unhappily, it was not to be.

FIRST GODCHILD

Linda Frisby Pamp was Grace Kelly's first godchild. Born in 1951, she was the daughter of Grace's friend Maree Frisby, known as "Friz." Grace had met her while both were students at Stevens, a small private interdenominational girls' school in Germantown. Maree was later chosen to be one of Grace's six bridesmaids.

FIRST NEWSPAPER REVIEW

Grace Kelly was sixteen when she made her professional acting debut with the East Falls Old Academy Players. Her leading role in her uncle George Kelly's *The Torch Bearers* elicited the following review in a Philadelphia newspaper: "The Kellys of East Falls have a new member making a bid for the limelight. Grace Kelly, John B's pretty daughter, made her pro stage debut last night in Uncle George Kelly's comedy hit, 'The Torch Bearers.' For a young lady whose previous experience was slim, Miss Kelly came through this footlight baptism of fire splendidly. Although father and mother beamed at Grace from the front row and other friends were scattered throughout the house, it was largely a theatrical crowd this girl faced on her break-in. From where we sat, it appeared as if Grace Kelly should become the theatrical torchbearer for her family."

THE FIRST PRINCE RAINIER

The first Prince Rainier, Lord of Monaco, was born in 1267 and died in 1314. A painting that shows him wearing the chain mail and helmet of a warrior of the period is on display at the royal palace in Monte Carlo.

FIRST ROYAL FUNERAL BY SATELLITE

Princess Grace's funeral was the first royal funeral to be telecast by satellite. An estimated one hundred million people worldwide watched the services live.

FIRST SUNDAY IN MONACO

On Sunday, April 15, 1956, Grace Kelly attended early morning Mass in the small Palatine Chapel in the royal palace. Twenty-six years later her body would lie in state in the very same chapel.

FIRST TELEVISION DRAMA

Celebrated 1950s producer Fred Coe cast Grace Kelly in her first television drama, "Beth Meriday," in 1949. It was adapted from a short story by famed novelist Sinclair Lewis. Coe described her as having style. "She wasn't just another beautiful girl; she was the essence of freshness, the kind of girl every man dreams of marrying."

THE FIRST THING RAINIER SHOWED GRACE

After welcoming Grace Kelly to his palace the day they met, the first thing Prince Rainier showed his guest was his pet tiger.

During Grace's first meeting with Rainier in April 1955, the Prince gave her a tour of his private zoo and introduced her to his pet tiger. (Edward Quinn/Globe Photos)

It was but one of a large collection of wild animals the prince kept in his private zoo on the palace grounds.

FIRST TIME IN A BATHING SUIT

In *The Bridges at Toko-Ri* (1954), Grace Kelly made her first screen appearance in a bathing suit. Playing navy pilot William Holden's wife, she spends one last week with him in Tokyo before he goes on a dangerous mission. Their swimming scene prompted *Time* magazine to comment that the film established the fact that she had a better figure than expected. Her second and last appearance in a bathing suit occurred two years later in *High Society*, when she and Frank Sinatra take a romantic swim on the eve of her marriage to John Lund.

FITNESS ADVOCATE

Jack Kelly was actively concerned with the health of American children. He wrote an article titled "Are We Becoming a Nation of Weaklings?" for the March 1956 issue of *American* magazine that was later reprinted in *Reader's Digest*. According to Grace's father, "American youngsters today are weaker and flabbier than those in many other countries, and they are growing softer every year. Their physical fitness or lack of it constitutes one of our gravest problems. If parents and teachers fail to wake up to the alarming trend, we shall become a nation of weaklings."

Although Grace tried to be athletic as a child, she tended to be more bookish and introverted than her siblings.

FORESHADOWING HER DEATH

Grace Kelly was a notoriously bad driver. During the filming of *To Catch a Thief* in the south of France, a scene with Cary Grant called for her to drive furiously and rapidly along the dangerous mountain roads. Since there was no way to fake the scene or use a double, Hitchcock and crew—and Cary Grant—held their respective breaths. At one point Grace almost lost control and managed to slam on the brakes only at the edge of a precipice on a winding road similar to the one on which she had her fatal crash twenty-seven years later.

A FRAIL, SICKLY GIRL

As a child Grace was the frail, sickly one in a family of athletic overachievers. She suffered from repeated colds, acute sore throats, asthma, and hay fever. She had measles twice, chicken pox, and at least one serious bout with pneumonia.

LISA CAROL FREMONT

The name of Grace Kelly's character in *Rear Window* was Lisa Carol Fremont, the wealthy, sophisticated girlfriend of photog-

The liberated sophisticated woman, circa 1954, Grace Kelly as Rear Window's *Lisa Fremont, who literally moves in on the helpless man she loves, James Stewart.*

rapher James Stewart. He was wheelchair-bound in his Greenwich Village apartment after breaking his leg and relieved his boredom by spying on his neighbors through his telephoto lens. As Lisa, Grace was elegant and controlled but also quick to take advantage of her boyfriend's situation. Knowing full well his leg cast prevented him from moving, she paraded before him in a revealing nightgown, provocatively remarking, "Preview of coming attraction." Her attempts to woo him into proposing marriage were lighthearted and charming until he convinced her a man had murdered his wife in an apartment across the courtyard. That's when Lisa changed from a brittle sophisticate into a resourceful helpmate. One of the film's most memorable scenes showed a determined Lisa scampering up a ladder and into the murderer's apartment while James Stewart watched in helpless horror as the murderer returned.

THE FRENCH GRACE KELLY

New Yorker film critic Pauline Kael once described French film star Catherine Deneuve as "the French Grace Kelly."

FRENCH WITH TEARS

With her usual concentration and diligence, Grace learned to speak French well enough for official occasions and formal speeches. Her accent was deemed superb, but her command of the nuances of the language was lacking. It embarrassed and frustrated her that she could not express the subtleties of thought and opinion that she could in English.

Having avoided press interviews in French because of this inadequacy, she finally felt ready to do a radio interview in French about her various cultural projects that she hoped would be of interest to French listeners. The French interviewer was charming and easygoing in his approach, but within minutes Grace had to cancel out. The words she wanted simply refused to come. Tearful and upset by this failure, Grace the Perfectionist vowed never to attempt such an interview again.

"THE FRIENDLY FLORIST"

Oleg Cassini's courtship of Grace Kelly began with an anonymous barrage of red roses, a dozen of the long stems delivered daily for ten days with an accompanying card signed simply "The Friendly Florist."

CLARK GABLE

Clark Gable was newly divorced from British socialite Lady Sylvia Ashley and deeply involved with French model Suzanne Dadolle in 1953 when he arrived in Africa for *Mogambo* and met Grace Kelly. She was young, blond, and bore a passing resemblance to his late wife, Carole Lombard, who had died in a plane crash during World War II. Joan Crawford said Grace lacked Carole's sophistication, wit, salty tongue, and spunk. "But I was sure Clark would be attracted to the prim young thing. He had just gone through a dreadful divorce, and MGM wasn't going to renew his contract. He was a big lonely lug who drank too much. Clark was on a binge when he married Lady Ashley and I was worried he might do the same damn thing with Kelly."

Gable did indeed fall in love with Grace Kelly, and their romance flourished amid the intensity of making the film and the dangers of Africa. Grace desperately wanted to marry him, insisting the nearly thirty-year age difference didn't matter.

Back in London after their idyllic weeks in Africa, an affectionate, almost paternal Clark Gable accompanied Grace to the airport for her flight back to America. Ignoring the shouts of photographers and reporters, he embraced her fondly and kissed her good-bye. Sobbing miserably, she rushed blindly through the gate to the New York–bound plane. A few weeks later Gable was again seen in Paris with his longtime French lover, model Suzanne Dadolle.

Clark Gable caught between Grace Kelly and Ava Gardner, the two women who are in love with him in Mogambo.

When he finally returned to California in December, 1953, Gable found a Christmas gift from Grace Kelly, a tiny Mexican burro named "Ba," her nickname for him. They spoke by phone, and he promised to escort her to the Academy Awards in March. Grace had been nominated for best supporting actress in *Mogambo* but lost out to Donna Reed in *From Here to Eternity.*

Their reunion finally resolved their personal situation. Gable convinced her that though he loved her she was far too young for him and marriage was out of the question. Could they continue to be "just friends"? After a few casual dates the friendship petered out. There is no record of Clark's being invited to Grace's wedding or of the two ever meeting again in Monaco or elsewhere.

Brief Bio: Born William Clark Gable on February 1, 1901, in Cadiz, Ohio, he was the son of an oil driller. He left home at fourteen to work in a tire factory in nearby Akron, where he saw his first play and decided to become an actor. His ambition was delayed when his father got him a job in the Oklahoma oil fields. At twenty-one he joined a traveling troupe headed by veteran actress Josephine Dillon, who coached the young man and moved with him to Hollywood, where they married in 1924. Rejected for film roles, Gable had better success on Broadway, where he played romantic leads. Back in Hollywood, Darryl F. Zanuck said, "His ears are too big. He looks like an ape." This perception led to Gable being cast as thugs, villains, and tough guys in films opposite Norma Shearer, Greta Garbo, and Joan Crawford. Director Frank Capra then recognized his comedic and romantic possibilities and cast him opposite Claudette Colbert in the 1934 Academy Award–winning smash, *It Happened One Night.* Gable made close to thirty movies over the next five years before starring as Rhett Butler in *Gone With the Wind* in 1939. At the height of his popularity he was also at his happiest personally with his marriage to Carole Lombard. Their "match made in heaven" ended tragically in 1942, when the plane carrying her home from a war bond drive crashed into a mountain. The bereaved widower joined the U.S. Air Force, rising from lieutenant to major and receiving the Distinguished Flying Cross and Air Medal for flying bombing missions over Germany.

Postwar, he costarred with Doris Day, Gene Tierney, Greer Garson, Ava Gardner, and Grace Kelly. In his final film, *The Misfits*, he played opposite Marilyn Monroe, who once confessed that she had fantasized as a child that Gable was her father. The strain of doing his own stunts aggravated a heart condition and led to his death on November 16, 1960. He did not live to see his good reviews or his first and only child, John Clark Gable, who was born a short time later. Of his five wives, the first two, Josephine Dillon and Rhea Langham, were respectively fourteen and seventeen years older than he. Seven years after Carole Lombard's fatal crash, he married former actress Lady Sylvia Ashley, who had been married to Douglas Fairbanks. It didn't last. In 1955 he married a woman who had loved him for years and finally got his attention, Kay Spreckels, who was pregnant with his son when he died. In 1976 he was portrayed on screen by actor James Brolin in *Gable and Lombard*.

RITA GAM ON GRACE

Close friend and bridesmaid Rita Gam said in tribute to Grace after her death, "Her strength to be constant, loyal, and de-

Grace Kelly at her devotions, a candid shot of her attending Mass.

pendable came from the Catholic Church. Her reverence for the church started at home."

RITA GAM'S FIRST IMPRESSION OF GRACE

In the 1987 TV documentary, "Grace Kelly: The American Princess," Rita Gam recalled her first meeting with Grace Kelly in 1948. "The first time I saw Grace, I would be hard-pressed to describe her as the glamour queen of the world. She had a pair of glasses on and they were a little bit down her nose. And she had a terrible cold and she was quite withdrawn. I remember we shook hands. But it wasn't a very hearty handshake. It was the handshake of a little girl. And I thought, 'Oh, what a nice school teacher. She's from Philadelphia!' "

A GARELLI MOTORBIKE

Prince Albert inherited a love of vehicles from his father, who maintains a large collection. At the Grimaldi family's seventeenth-century hunting lodge, Château de Marchais, seventy-five miles north of Paris, Albert enjoys riding a red and black Garelli motorbike.

"A GENTLEMAN AND A SCULLER"

A popular quip about John B. Kelly in the Philadelphia of the 1930s was "a gentleman and a sculler." The jest referred to his winning an Olympic gold medal as a champion sculler—after being denied the right to compete in Britain's Henley Regatta because he was "not a gentleman."

KAHLIL GIBRAN'S "LIVING ARROWS"

Asked to share her secrets of child rearing in 1974, Princess Grace told McCall's magazine, "I love the way Kahlil Gibran says it in The Prophet, that children are living arrows that the parents send into the world." What she wanted for her own "arrows" was "that they become responsible people, with character—strong, able to take it, yet also understanding of the weak. That they may be good sports and play the game according to the rules. But life's also a game of broken rules—and to be prepared for that, too."

A GIFT FROM HER NEW FATHER-IN-LAW

As a wedding gift to Grace, Prince Rainier's father, Count Polignac, presented her with a family heirloom necklace that had belonged to Rainier's great grandmother. It was an enormous pearl surrounded by rubies attached to a gold chain by a diamond filigree crown.

GIGI AND THE MONTE CARLO CONNECTION

In one of fate's ironies, Grace Kelly auditioned for the title role in the Broadway production of Colette's famous work but was turned down. Subsequently Colette saw Audrey Hepburn on a film location in Monte Carlo in 1951 and recommended her for the role. Five years later Grace Kelly moved to Monte Carlo in the title role of Her Serene Highness. If she had played Gigi on Broadway, her career and personal life might have been totally different. (Audrey Hepburn turned down the screen role; Leslie Caron, who had played Gigi in London, accepted and won international fame.)

GIRL SCOUTS CAMP OUT WITH CAROLINE

A year after her mother's death, a still-grieving Princess Caroline assumed her responsibilities as head of the Monaco Girl Scouts. At the end of August 1983 she put on her scout uniform and accompanied fifty-six young members of the Monte Carlo chapter to the Grimaldi family estate, the Château de Marchais, north of Paris. Led by their twenty-six-year-old princess, the youngsters camped out and practiced the many wholesome disciplines of scouting.

The troop had a wonderful time. For Caroline the expedition took her mind off her sorrow and helped her endure the long healing process that still lay ahead.

GIVING A HAND TO HANDICRAFTS

Princess Grace gave a helping hand to local craftspeople in Monaco by sponsoring a number of boutiques under the auspices of the Princess Grace Foundation. After her death in 1982 the boutiques continued their good work of offering the handicrafts of more than sixty artists, many of them handicapped, to visiting tourists at moderate prices.

GOOD REVIEWS FOR RAYMOND MASSEY'S "DAUGHTER"

Actor/director Raymond Massey auditioned twenty-one actresses before casting Grace Kelly in *The Father*, the Strindberg drama about a man driven mad by his wife's insinuations that their daughter is not his.

After a Boston tryout the play opened at New York's Cort Theater on November 16, 1949. The *New York Times* enthused, "Grace Kelly gives a charming, pliable performance as the bewildered broken-hearted daughter." Critic George Jean Nathan called "the novice Grace Kelly convincing as the daughter."

The Father ran for sixty-nine performances—not exactly a hit but not a flop either—and it did give Grace some invaluable professional experience.

GPK COLLAGES

In the late 1970s Princess Grace's passion for flowers and flower arranging developed into a new means of artistic expression; she created collages from pressed flowers. What began as a hobby soon developed into an art. In 1977, she had her first one-woman show at the Galerie Drouant in Paris. Signing her work GPK (for Grace Patricia Kelly) instead of Grace de Monaco, she enjoyed the artist's pleasure of seeing her work sell out.

As biographer Steven Englund explains, Grace followed no set methods in her collages and used no prior designs. Instead of the corrugated cardboard recommended for pressing flowers, she used old phone books. "After pressing them for a month, Grace would excitedly lay them out . . . and start to improvise, fitting petals, leaves and stems in whatever way suited her impulse." Her pressed flowers included primroses, periwinkles, jasmine, daisies, forget-me-nots, hydrangeas, and Queen Anne's lace. *My Book of Flowers*, an illustrated book of her designs co-written with Gwen Robyns, was published in 1980. In 1978, the Springmaid fabric company presented the Springmaid–Grace Kelly Pressed Flower Collection of sheets, pillowcases, bed-spreads, draperies, and dust ruffles for the bedroom as well as a separate group of table linens. The only sour note to the enterprise was the comment by the *Village Voice*, a weekly newspaper in New York, which called flower pressing "the most depressing art form known to man" and described the slide show of Princess Grace in Monaco as "meandering through the mountains with a basket in her hand like a de-mented Heidi . . . squatting over a half-dead flower."

GRACE AND CARY SHARE A MOVIE MOM

The stylish, witty, and often zany Jessie Royce Landis brought a new dimension to sophisticated movie motherhood in the 1950s. She played Grace Kelly's mother in *To Catch a Thief* and *The Swan* in 1955 and 1956 respectively. In 1959 she played Cary Grant's mother in *North by Northwest*. She and Grace maintained an ongoing friendship until the older woman's death in 1972 at the age of sixty-eight.

GRACE AND MARIA AS THE TWO MARYS?

One fine day in the early 1960s, Grace and Rainier were cruis-ing on the Aristotle Onassis yacht with the shipping tycoon and his mistress Maria Callas when a cable arrived from Spyros Skouras. He was planning to film *The Greatest Story Ever Told* and was offering a million dollars to Grace if she would play the Virgin Mary and another million to Maria if she would be Mary Magdalene. The offer was greeted with hilarity by the two women and the men in their lives.

GRACE AND RAINIER "PARACHUTE" TO EARTH

During the fireworks display celebrating their marriage enormous "portraits" of Grace and Rainier were fired by rockets high into the night sky above Monaco. They lingered for a moment to the cheers of the crowds below before floating to the ground attached to small parachutes.

GRACE AS A BRIDESMAID

Grace Kelly's younger sister, Lizanne, was attending the University of Pennsylvania in the early 1950s when she met Donald LeVine, a lifeguard and former football star of Bethany College. The courtship began in Ocean City, the New Jersey seaside resort where the Kellys and LeVines spent their summers.

On June 1, 1955, Lizanne graduated from the university. Three weeks later, on her birthday, June 25, she and Don were married at St. Bridget's Church in the Falls of Schuylkill, the Kelly family parish. Peggy was maid of honor, Kell an usher, and Grace a bridesmaid.

GRACE AT CHARLES AND DIANA'S WEDDING

Wearing ivory silk and a cocoa-brown straw hat, Princess Grace attended the July 1981 royal wedding of Prince Charles and Lady Diana. Little more than a year later, the princess of Wales represented the British royal family at Princess Grace's funeral in Monaco.

GRACE INFURIATES THE COMMUNIST *DAILY WORKER*

Grace Kelly's choice of a husband made Joseph North of America's official Communist Party newspaper the *Daily Worker* froth at the mouth. How could the daughter of a laboring man choose a mate "who can't lay bricks . . . or act . . . or write plays . . . or row a boat?"

GRACE LOSES HER *CYRANO* ROLE

In 1950 famed producer Jean Dalrymple suggested Grace Kelly for the role of Roxanne in the City Center production of *Cyrano de Bergerac*. Leading man Jose Ferrer responded with a series of vehement *nos*. She was an amateur, he couldn't hear her while she auditioned, and he didn't think she was ready for such a demanding role. Ferrer won. Grace lost the role and moved on. A sorely disappointed Dalrymple recalled Grace's youthful beauty and fragility many years later. "I love her gentleness and her lovely cultivated voice and speech, and thought she was ideal for the Lady Roxanne."

GRACE LOVED *HENRY*

Rainier didn't. When their son was born in 1958, he was christened Albert plus several more names, none of them Henry. Grace's fondness for Britain's Princess Diana undoubtedly would have grown when Diana named her second son Henry— five years after Grace's death.

GRACE "NIBBLED"

In covering the first public appearance of Grace and Rainier after they announced their engagement, *Time* magazine said that the actress "nibbled crystallized violets" at the Night in Monte Carlo charity ball at New York's Waldorf-Astoria and that a little while later she "nibbled at Rainier's ear" while dancing at the Harwyn Club.

GRACE PROPOSES TO OLEG

The setting was the south of France, a small fish restaurant in Cannes, the year 1954. Grace Kelly and Oleg Cassini had been a serious romance for many months when, according to Cassini in his autobiography, *In My Fashion*, she said, "I want to make my life with you. I want to be your wife."

Grace with Oleg Cassini and Alfred Hitchcock at the premiere of Rear Window *in August 1954.* (UPI/Bettmann)

GRACE REMEMBERS AVA'S BIRTHDAY

On January 24, 1954, Ava Gardner's thirty-second birthday, she was on location in Africa with *Mogambo*. Costar Grace Kelly helped to arrange a birthday party in the jungle, and for years afterward she sent Ava a birthday present on her natal day.

GRACE SAYS "I DO" TO GARY COOPER

In *High Noon*, Grace Kelly's first words to Gary Cooper are "I do" when as the shy young Quaker she marries him in a simple ceremony.

THE GRACE VS. AVA RIVALRY

According to the newspaper ads promoting *Mogambo* in 1953, Clark Gable's two leading ladies, Grace Kelly and Ava Gardner, were at each other's throat. "They fought like jungle cats! A flaming love feud! The jungle strips two civilized women of all but their most primeval instincts!"

The truth is they became good friends and maintained the friendship until Grace's death.

GRACE WANTED IT; LIZ GOT IT

Grace Kelly wanted the role of Leslie in *Giant* (1956), but director George Stevens preferred Elizabeth Taylor. The old rivalry was long forgotten by the time Liz and husband Richard Burton attended Princess Grace's fortieth birthday celebration in Monaco in 1969.

GRACE WINS OVER JUDY BY SEVEN VOTES

The competition for the best actress Oscar in 1954 was said to be between Grace Kelly for *The Country Girl* and Judy Garland for *A Star Is Born*. Conventional wisdom predicted a Garland win for the sentimental reason that she had just had a baby and would be awaiting the announcement in her hospital bed.

When Grace Kelly won, columnist Hedda Hopper called it the closest Oscar race ever that didn't result in a tie. Using all of her sources to find out what happened, the columnist concluded that Grace had won by a mere seven votes. "And you know where those seven votes were, don't you? They belonged to those bastards in the front office at MGM."

GRACELESS JOKES IN THE PRESS

Hit unexpectedly by the sudden announcement of Grace and Rainier's engagement, press columnists hit back with decidedly limp attempts at humor. *New York Daily News* columnist Robert Sylvester asked, "Will the towels at the royal palace in Monaco be marked 'His and Heirs'?"

In Chicago, Irv Kupcinet of the *Sun-Times* remarked, "It isn't the romance that interests Miss Kelly—it's the *principality* of the thing."

As for United Press International, Aline Mosby informed readers all over the country, "MGM's executives are worried Grace will fly off to Monte Carlo and be seen henceforth only on postage stamps!"

GRACE'S CHILDREN ARE MULTILINGUAL

Growing up in Monaco, Caroline, Albert, and Stephanie spoke English with their mother, spoke French with their father, and studied German, Italian, and Spanish. Like many well-educated Europeans, they are able to switch from one language to another with ease.

GRACE'S DOLL COLLECTION

Grace Kelly's younger sister, Lizanne, remembered how carefully Grace took care of her doll collection when they were children. Years later, visiting the palace in Monaco, Lizanne looked in a closet and saw every one of her sister's old dolls. Grace expressed surprise that Lizanne had not kept hers.

GRACE'S FINAL RESTING PLACE

On September 21, 1982, Princess Grace was laid to rest in the Grimaldi family vault in the Cathedral of St. Nicholas twenty-six years and five months after marrying Prince Rainier in the same place. Visitors may read the inscription on white marble that says simply, "Grace Patricia, wife of Prince Rainier III, died the year of our Lord, 1982."

GRACE'S FIRST LOVE

She was fourteen. Harper Davis was two years older, a student at Penn Charter, an old established school attended by Grace's brother, Kell, and other Germantown friends. Their friendship was a close one and continued for several years. Kelly family intimates have said the two youngsters were serious and the relationship could have led to marriage. But in 1946 Harper contracted multiple sclerosis; he died six years later. Grace visited him frequently in the hospital. At his death in 1953 she canceled her Hollywood schedule and flew to Philadelphia for his memorial service.

GRACE'S HEAD ON ANOTHER GIRL'S BODY

An MGM promotion poster for *Green Fire* combined Grace Kelly's head with an anonymous voluptuous body draped in a clinging green gown. Grace avoided Times Square where the poster was on display. "It makes me so mad. And the dress isn't even in the picture."

GRACE'S HOMETOWN PRIEST

Father John Cartin, parish priest of the Kelly family's Philadelphia church, St. Bridget's, was in attendance at the Grace-Rainier wedding.

GRACE'S KIDS NEVER "HOME ALONE"

In recent years Britain's Princess of Wales has taken her children on official trips abroad, seen by many as a revolutionary

Grace felt strongly about being a mother first and, accordingly, her children received the lion's share of her time, often accompanying her to public engagements and trips abroad. (Rex Features London)

change in royal family protocol. Few remember that it was Princess Grace and Prince Rainier who set this precedent.

As early as 1959, when President Charles de Gaulle invited them to Paris on a state visit, Caroline and Albert went, too. In between official duties, Prince Rainier made time to take them to the Bois de Boulogne, the famous Paris park, and push them on the public swings.

"GRACE'S PLACE"

British actor and author Dirk Bogarde called Monte Carlo "Grace's Place."

GRANDDAUGHTER OF IRISH IMMIGRANTS

More than a hundred years after her Kelly grandparents immigrated to America from county Mayo, Princess Grace and her husband paid a state visit to Ireland. John Fitzgerald Kennedy had just been inaugurated as president of the United States. Irish pride was reaching hysteria when Grace and Rainier arrived at the Dublin airport early in 1961.

In honor of the occasion Grace wore a Kelly green suit designed by Christian Dior, so there was no mistaking her when the estimated crowd of twenty thousand surged toward her shouting, "Grace! Grace!"

What seemed like the entire population lined the road to O'Connell Street in Dublin's "fair city" where President and Mrs. Eamon De Valera waited to officially greet the royal visitors at the Gresham Hotel. One tense moment came when the excited crowd rocked the Rolls-Royce in which they were riding. Panic erupted, and fifty people were shaken up in the struggle to restore order. According to the *Irish Times*, Grace was escorted into the hotel visibly upset but soon recovered her poise sufficiently to appear on the balcony to acknowledge the waiting crowd's cries, "We want Grace."

As one journalist commented, "Everyone here has discovered their name is Kelly!"

The sentimental high point of the visit was the journey to Drumirla just outside Newport in county Mayo on the west coast, where Grace's grandfather John Henry Kelly had lived in a two-room cottage. Ownership of the cottage had passed to a white-haired widow, Ellen Mulchrone, who offered "the Kelly girl" and her prince buttered scones and strong Irish tea. She also told them about a fortune teller she had met many years before who had predicted, "A beautiful woman will visit you from Europe, and her all dripping in diamonds. . . ." Fifteen years later, when Mrs. Mulchrone died, Grace bought her "ancestral" home.

When President Kennedy visited Ireland in 1963, the population again went wild, only this time everyone seemed to be a Kennedy.

CARY GRANT

Cary Grant came out of retirement in 1955 to make *To Catch a Thief*. The chemistry between him and Grace Kelly was immediate and continued strong for the rest of her life. Their love scenes were sophisticated and sexy by implication. Grant's theory about love scenes was that the man should always allow the woman to come to him. In *To Catch a Thief*, Grace Kelly's sexual overtures to him were playful and witty as well as sexy.

To his great disappointment, he and wife Betsy Drake could not attend Grace's wedding the following year because he was filming *The Pride and the Passion* in Spain. They sent an antique desk as a wedding gift and a few weeks later met up with the honeymooners in Spain.

In July 1956 Betsy was among the passengers on the Italian liner *Andrea Doria*, which sank in a collision off the coast of Nantucket. Cary had flown back to America while his wife had chosen to enjoy a quiet sea voyage while she worked on a book she was writing. She was among the 1,134 people rescued. Her baggage had gone down with the sinking ship, but her only regret was the loss of the film footage she had taken of Grace and Rainier in Spain.

Cary's friendship with Grace continued through the several changes in his personal life. His marriage to Betsy ended in divorce on August 14, 1962. His next marriage, to actress Dyan Cannon, lasted only three years but produced a daughter, Jennifer. His last marriage, to Barbara Harris, brought him the contentment that had previously eluded him.

Rumors of a continuing love affair with Grace began with *To Catch a Thief*. Their love scenes sizzled, but an off-screen dalliance at that time seems unlikely since his wife Betsy Drake and her lover Oleg Cassini were there as well. What's more, when the cast flew to Hollywood to complete the film, Grace spent her weekends with Cary and his wife at the Hitchcock place near Santa Cruz. That's where the Grants presented her with the miniature black poodle, Oliver.

In 1961 rumors of an affair were fueled by Princess Grace's invitation to Cary and Betsy to spend Easter with the Grimaldis in Monaco. Excited at seeing her old friends, Grace met them at

Cary Grant came out of retirement to play John Robie "the cat" opposite Grace Kelly in To Catch a Thief *in 1955.*

Nice airport but with no formal fanfare. A photographer caught her in the act of kissing Cary hello and then cropped out his wife, who had been standing beside him, causing a minor sulk from Rainier when the picture appeared worldwide.

This didn't end the friendship. After Dyan Cannon divorced him, Cary frequently visited Monaco with his daughter and kept in touch with Grace by phone, mail, and personal visits when possible.

Anonymous gossips have sworn that Princess Grace sought solace from the loneliness of middle age with Cary Grant and that they met in London and Paris for secret trysts. It's possible, of course, but difficult to believe that two instantly recognizable people could totally elude prying eyes and cameras.

When Princess Caroline married Philippe Junot in June 1978, Cary Grant was among Grace's Hollywood crowd who gathered in Monaco in support, including the David Nivens, the Gregory Pecks, the Frank Sinatras, and Ava Gardner. His final "visit" with Grace was at her funeral in September 1982. He and his wife Barbara were the only Hollywood mourners in attendance. Although David Niven lived nearby, by then he was too seriously ill to appear. Upon learning of Grace's death, Cary Grant said, "It hit me so hard because it was so horribly, horribly unexpected."

Knowing she was dead was one thing. Seeing her in her coffin was something else. The funeral was so overwhelming it was all he could do to retain a modicum of composure before breaking down in tears once he and Barbara reached the privacy of their car.

Brief Bio: Cary Grant was born Archibald Alexander Leach on January 18, 1904, in Bristol, England, in a poverty-stricken environment. At thirteen he joined a traveling acrobatic troupe as a song-and-dance man and juggler. When the troupe arrived in New York in 1920, he decided to seek his fortune in America. After three years as a Coney Island lifeguard, stilt-walker and small-time vaudeville performer, he finally appeared in a Broadway musical, *Golden Dawn.*

By 1932 he had arrived in Hollywood, where some of the screen's reigning beauties chose the neophyte as costar and launched his career. He was Marlene Dietrich's lover in *Blonde Venus* and Mae West's costar in *She Done Him Wrong,* in which she made her immortal invitation to him, "Come up and see me sometime."

Soon his flair for screwball comedy cast Grant opposite Constance Bennett, Irene Dunne, and Katharine Hepburn, leading to meatier roles opposite Ingrid Bergman, Loretta Young, Myrna Loy, Deborah Kerr, Sophia Loren, Audrey Hep-

Grace maintained a close friendship with Cary Grant all her life. They visited each other often and spent several vacations together, including this one in Las Vegas in 1955 with Cary's wife, Betsy Drake, and Ray Bolger. (UPI/Bettmann)

burn—and, for Alfred Hitchcock, opposite Grace Kelly and Eva Marie Saint.

Grant's first four marriages ended disastrously. First wife

Virginia Cherrill had played the blind flower girl in Chaplin's *City Lights* and eventually married the ninth earl of Jersey. Next came a three-year marriage to Woolworth heiress Barbara Hutton during World War II, followed by a ten-year marriage to actress Betsy Drake. He was a bachelor for nearly ten years until his 1965 marriage to Dyan Cannon, who bore him a daughter when he was past sixty.

Apart from his loving friendship with Grace, which lasted more than a quarter of a century, his other great love was Sophia Loren, whom he met filming *The Pride and the Passion* and later costarred with in *Houseboat*. He and Sophia had discussed marriage, but she chose to stay with her mentor, Carlo Ponti, marrying him by proxy from Mexico during the filming of *Houseboat*.

In one of fate's ironies, Cary and Sophia did "marry" in the film. As Loren recalled, "I was a radiant bride dressed in a long white gown of antique lace and carrying a bouquet of white roses. . . . Mendelssohn's wedding music was playing and Cary was waiting for me at the altar with a white carnation in his buttonhole. I was aware of how painful it was for him to play this scene with me, to have the minister pronounce us man and wife, to take me in his arms and kiss me. It was painful for me, too."

Although he and Sophia did not continue their friendship over the years as had he and Grace, Grant's death on November 29, 1986, prompted Loren to film a message of condolence from her home in Rome that was shown to those gathered in Hollywood in his memory.

On October 19, 1988, in the presence of Rainier, Albert, and Stephanie, the Princess Grace Foundation paid tribute to Cary Grant at a thousand-dollar-a-plate dinner at the Beverly Hilton Hotel in Beverly Hills. Nearly a million dollars was raised for a scholarship fund for young people in film, theater, and dance. Among those who "sang for their supper" were Michael Caine, Quincy Jones, Frank Sinatra, Gregory Peck, James Stewart, and Liza Minnelli. Honorary chairpersons of the event were Barbara Grant and Nancy Reagan. Also in attendance was Judy Balaban Quine, one of Princess Grace's brides-maids and oldest friends.

CARY GRANT ON GRACE

After filming *To Catch a Thief*, Cary Grant said of his costar, "Grace had a kind of serenity, a calmness, that I hadn't arrived at at that point of my life—and perhaps never will, for all I know. She was so relaxed in front of the camera that she made it look simple.

"She made acting look as easy as Frank Sinatra made singing appear. Everyone thinks they can sing after an evening at the theater listening to Frank, but to create the sense of ease takes a tremendous amount of knowledge and experience and talent.

"Grace was astonishing. When you played a love scene with her, she really listened. She was right there with you. She was Buddha-like in her concentration. She was like Garbo in that respect."

CARY GRANT'S POODLE'S BROTHER

Oliver, the black poodle Grace Kelly carried in her arms on the day in 1956 that she arrived in Monaco to marry Prince Rainier, was given to her by Cary Grant and his wife at that time, Betsy Drake. Oliver was the brother of their poodle, April.

KATHRYN GRANT'S JEALOUSY

After Bing Crosby's death in 1977, his widow, actress Kathryn Grant, told Princess Grace, "I've been jealous of you for the entire twenty years of our marriage. Bing always loved you."

THE GREEN CHRYSLER IMPERIAL

Upon her arrival in Monaco in April 1956, Grace Kelly was greeted by her husband-to-be aboard his yacht, the *Deo Juvante*

II. Once ashore, he escorted her to his waiting green Chrysler Imperial for the ceremonial procession from the harbor to the palace.

THE GRIMALDI CHILDREN WERE "SEEN AND HEARD"

As parents Grace and Rainier rejected the aristocratic tradition of consigning children to the care of nursemaids and seeing very little of them. The children often traveled with them on state visits and even when very young attended receptions and exhibitions. Surprisingly, Grace was extremely permissive and did little to stop them when their behavior became disruptive.

According to onetime lady-in-waiting Madge Tivey-Faucon, Caroline could twist her mother around her little finger. And Grace could never resist Caroline's tears. At the first sob, especially at bedtime, Grace would delay her departure for an evening event until the little girl fell asleep. More and more often she avoided upsets by taking Caroline and Albert with her.

THE "GRIMALDI CURSE"

According to Grimaldi family legend, Prince Rainier's thirteenth-century ancestor, the first Prince Rainier, was known for his triumphs as a sailor and a lover. Although his naval exploits won him the honor of being admiral general of France, his betrayal of a Flemish princess resulted in her cursing him and all who would follow: "Never will a Grimaldi find true happiness in marriage!"

Rainier's parents and grandparents did in fact suffer extreme marital discord. However, regarding his own marriage to Grace Kelly, Rainier said, "We fooled the curse!" Their twenty-six-year marriage was solid, fruitful, and happy.

GRIMALDI "FAMILY PICNIC" FOR FIVE THOUSAND MONEGASQUES

To celebrate Prince Rainier's twenty-fifth anniversary as Monaco's reigning prince in 1974, he and Princess Grace invited the entire native Monégasque population of some five thousand citizens to a family-style picnic in the Monte Carlo soccer stadium.

ALEC GUINNESS AND THE TOMAHAWK

If ever proof was needed of Grace Kelly's sense of humor, the "tomahawk" episode is it. As Judith Balaban Quine tells it the fun began in Asheville, North Carolina, where *The Swan* was on location. Jessie Royce Landis, who had played Grace's mother in *To Catch a Thief*, reprised that role this time as Princess Alexandra's mom. At one point during the filming "Roycie" visited a nearby Indian reservation in the Great Smoky Mountains and returned with a tomahawk as a souvenir gift for Alec Guinness.

Since he was leaving the next day and didn't want to bother with the cumbersome eighteen-inch object, he tipped one of the staff to slip it into Grace's bed. Nothing was ever said, and Guinness had long forgotten the incident when some

Grace and Alec Guinness inspect visiting cameraman Josh Weiner's equipment on the set of The Swan. *(Globe Photos)*

years later, long after Grace had married Rainier, he found the tomahawk in his bed in his cottage in the English countryside.

From then on the game continued, though neither Grace nor Alec ever mentioned it.

In 1978 the tomahawk turned up in Princess Grace's bed in Minneapolis during a poetry reading tour with Britain's Royal Shakespeare Company actor Richard Pasco. When she asked Pasco if perchance he knew Guinness, the actor could truthfully say no. Clearly some mutual friend had made the arrangements. True to the "tomahawk" code, she never mentioned her find.

Princess Grace waited patiently for her opportunity. Upon learning that Sir Alec would be receiving a Life Achievement Oscar in 1980, she arranged for the tomahawk to be sent by messenger to her good friend Rupert Allan. When Guinness returned to the Beverly Wilshire Hotel after the ceremonies, there was the tomahawk in his bed.

The final episode of the long-running joke took place the following year in Chichester, England, where Princess Grace was doing a poetry reading. She had packed light, and when she opened her overnight bag, there was the tomahawk raffishly painted with daisies, nestled in her underwear.

Her death a year later ended the thirty-year game. The whereabouts of the tomahawk remain a mystery.

PHILIPPE HALSMAN, PHOTOGRAPHER

His "come hither" cover portrait of Grace Kelly in 1954 heralded what *Life* magazine called "A Year of Grace." In three-quarters profile, her hair over one eye, her expression sexually provocative yet ladylike, the photograph established Grace's unique star quality. Two years earlier, a Halsman cover photograph of Marilyn Monroe had given a similar impetus to her burgeoning career.

"THE HANDSOMEST MAN IN AMERICA"

President Franklin D. Roosevelt described his good friend Jack Kelly as "the handsomest man in America." When Kelly ran for mayor of Philadelphia in 1934, hostile newspapers sneered at him as an Adonis. Nearsighted like his daughter Grace, he was too vain to appear in public wearing glasses. Despite FDR's support, Kelly lost the election, a fact he attributed to his being an Irish Catholic in a predominantly Protestant city. It would be twenty years before a Catholic became mayor of Philadelphia and nearly thirty before John F. Kennedy became America's first Roman Catholic president.

EDITH HEAD

The Academy Award–winning costume designer advised Alfred Hitchcock on Grace Kelly's wardrobe in *Dial M for Murder*, created the star's multifaceted attire for *To Catch a Thief*, and became a close personal friend of the actress. Grace turned to her for help in transforming herself into the drab, defeated Georgie Elgin in *The Country Girl*. Edith Head accompanied a nervous Grace Kelly to the 1955 Academy Awards. Many people, including Grace, expected Judy Garland to win for her performance in *A Star Is Born*, but Edith Head was betting on Grace.

Recalling the special challenge of clothing Grace Kelly to look both seductive and aristocratic in *To Catch a Thief*, she described the strapless gown she had designed for the big scene in the hotel room where Grace decides to tempt Cary, thinking he is a jewel thief, with an enormous diamond necklace at her throat:

"The gown had to have simple lines so that it did not detract from the necklace yet it had to emanate a haute couture quality that matched the expensive jewels." Furthermore, in the close-ups of the love scene, "There had to be enough fabric showing so that the audience knew Grace had clothes on."

One of Hollywood's preeminent costume designers, Edith Head cloaked her own background with mystery. Her birth date varied according to her whim, as did her place of birth. Some biographical sources say she was born in Los Angeles in 1904. One gives the improbably named Searchlight, Nevada, as her hometown. Whatever her birth year, she died on October 24, 1982, three months after Grace's fatal accident. Her memorial service was attended by Elizabeth Taylor, for whose costumes in *A Place in the Sun* she received an Oscar, and by Bette Davis, who gave the eulogy.

HEDDA HOPPING MAD

Grace Kelly's romance with Oleg Cassini infuriated Hollywood columnist Hedda Hopper, who called Cassini too "devilish" for the "ethereal Miss Kelly." Wondering in print why with all the good-looking men around Grace had fallen in love with him, Hedda concluded, "It must be his mustache." Himself infuriated, Cassini sent her a telegram: "Okay, Hedda, I give up. I'll shave mine if you shave yours."

HELEN OF TROY AND PARIS

For East Coast high society in the 1950s an invitation to the annual masked ball at multimillionaire Charles Shipman and Joan Whitney Payson's Long Island estate was proof of one's importance and celebrity. To dramatize their relationship, Cassini decided he and Grace would go as Helen of Troy and the lover who started the Trojan War, Paris, she in a long togalike gown of gold and a golden laurel tiara, he in a short Greek tunic, sandals, and helmet. He ruefully recalls not seeing too much of her at the ball. "She was besieged by a giddy assortment of Vanderbilts, Whitneys and Paysons." The ball took place during the summer of 1955. Less than six months later, Grace told Oleg she was going to marry Prince Rainier.

DR. EMILE HERVET

Dr. Hervet was the royal gynecologist who delivered Princess Caroline. He and two colleagues attended Grace at the palace on January 23, 1957. Expecting to give birth in early February, Grace had been told by Hervet that it might be sooner.

At 3:00 A.M., Her Serene Highness began labor and was taken to the delivery room that had been set up in the palace library. According to biographer James Spada, Prince Rainier, like fathers from every station in life in those days, waited in an adjoining room, chain-smoking and pacing up and down as the hours wore on.

Late in the morning he sent word to his sister, Princess Antoinette, and his mother-in-law, who had flown in from Philadelphia for the occasion. At 9:27 A.M., without anesthesia, Grace delivered a healthy eight-pound, three-ounce girl.

ALFRED HITCHCOCK

Grace Kelly made the three most important films of her career—*Dial M for Murder, Rear Window,* and *To Catch a Thief*—for director Alfred Hitchcock. It was Hitchcock who recognized what was in the 1950s a totally new style of film heroine, what he called "sexual elegance." Under his guidance Grace metamorphosed from the adulterous wife who was also a victim in *Dial M* to the stylishly aggressive socialite in hot pursuit of James Stewart in *Rear Window* and finally to the gorgeous, witty, and provocative heiress in equally hot pursuit of Cary Grant in *To Catch a Thief.*

As Grace said later, "Working with Hitchcock was a tremendous experience and a very enriching one. As an actor, I learned a tremendous amount about motion picture making. He gave me a great deal of confidence in myself."

According to Hitchcock biographer Donald Spoto, the director fell desperately in love with Grace and was deeply upset by her failure to respond in kind. His obsession with the exquisite blond ice goddess who was really a smoldering volcano of sexuality was reflected in the Grace Kelly "clones" he cast in later films: Kim Novak, Eva Marie Saint, and Tippi Hedren.

Grace's retirement from films did not stop Hitchcock from offering her the leading role in *Marnie* in 1962. The film was based on a novel by Winston Graham, its heroine described as "a puzzlement, an enigma, fearful and fascinating." She was terrified of physical contact with men. When one touched her, she became violent. Screenplay adapter Evan Hunter defined her pursuit of crime as a substitute for sex.

Six years after her marriage, Princess Grace had not given up the hope of returning to films. After reading the script, she showed it to her husband, expecting a negative response. To her amazement, Rainier gave his consent, stipulating that Hitchcock schedule the filming during the Grimaldis' vacation period so as not to interfere with Grace's official duties.

Grace Kelly and James Stewart in Rear Window.

On March 18, 1962, the announcement was made to the press and the public. Her Serene Highness would make a film for the esteemed director Alfred Hitchcock between the months of August and November. Unfortunately, the citizens of Monaco did not react to the idea as well as Prince Rainier had. They were, in fact, furious that their princess would be kissing a man on film. When the plot of *Marnie* became known, and the Monégasques learned Grace's part called for her being raped, they were even more incensed. Some accused her of deserting her new country while Prince Rainier was in the midst of delicate negotiations with France regarding the tax loopholes of French citizens and companies using Monaco as a way of avoiding taxes in France. During this period, France threatened to set up customs stations at Monaco's borders as an intimidation tactic that could destroy tourism and threaten the tiny nation's independence.

Compounding the situation was the reaction of Grace's former studio, MGM. In letters to Grace and Hitchcock, MGM pointed out that her old contract had four years to run. Although Hitchcock's lawyers contended that the seven years of her contract had expired, a nasty legal battle loomed. Besieged from all sides, she decided it would be undignified and harmful to Rainier if she persisted.

Hitchcock's disappointment was acute. In his determination to make *Marnie* without Grace, he cast the equally icy Tippi Hedren and tried to repeat his Pygmalion role with her in that project and later in *The Birds*. Tippi—who incidentally is the mother of actress Melanie Griffith—was good in her roles but suffered the insurmountable disadvantage of "not being Grace Kelly."

Brief Bio: Sir Alfred Hitchcock was born August 13, 1899, in London, England, the son of a poultry dealer. He studied engineering at the University of London but in 1920 decided the movies were for him. Starting out as a titles designer for silent films, he progressed to scenario writer and director. His first film was *The Pleasure Garden* (1925); his second, *The Lodger* (1926), established his talent for suspense. In 1929 his *Blackmail* was the first successful British talking picture, and by the time he directed his first Academy Award–winning film, *Rebecca*, in 1940, he was the "master" of his genre.

Among Hitchcock's most memorable films are *Suspicion* (1941) with Cary Grant and Joan Fontaine, *Spellbound* (1945) with Gregory Peck and Ingrid Bergman, *North by Northwest* (1959) with Cary Grant and Eva Marie Saint, *Vertigo* (1958) with

Princess Grace with her mentor, Alfred Hitchcock.

Kim Novak and James Stewart, and three that starred Grace Kelly. The terrifying *Psycho* (1960), starring Janet Leigh and Anthony Perkins, is said to have frightened three decades of shower takers into switching to baths (and then only when someone else was around).

TV viewers can still see reruns of the several mystery series Hitchcock produced, introduced, and usually directed in the black-and-white days of the 1950s and 1960s. In 1979 he was awarded the American Film Institute's Life Achievement Award, and in 1980, shortly before his death on April 29, he was knighted by Queen Elizabeth II.

Film buffs have long enjoyed spotting him in the fleeting personal appearances he made in most of his films. In *To Catch a Thief*, for instance, he is seen sitting next to Cary Grant on a bus. Perhaps the most written about of all film directors, he has been the subject of articles and books by such other noted filmmakers as François Truffaut and Peter Bogdanovich.

WILLIAM HOLDEN

The actor known as "The Golden Boy" from the title of his first movie of that name was on the rebound from a passionate affair with Audrey Hepburn, his *Sabrina* costar, when he met Grace Kelly in 1954. Having a wife and two children did not hinder his pursuit of the young actress cast as his wife in *The Bridges at Toko-Ri*. Their brief romance might have wound up as "just one of those flings" if not for their being thrown together in the more emotionally intense plot of *The Country Girl*, in which the initial antagonisms turn into a love of overwhelming proportions.

Adding fuel to the fire was the presence on the set of Bing Crosby, a previous lover who was still very much enamored of Grace—and told Holden about it! Scandal clouds loomed when whispered rumors of Holden-Kelly intimacy reached the press. Grace's earlier affair with *Dial M* costar Ray Milland had branded her a homewrecker. Sightings of Bill Holden's instantly recognizable white Cadillac Eldorado convertible outside her Sweetzer Avenue apartment in Hollywood started tongues wagging in earnest. He was quoted as saying, "I love Grace and want to marry her."

According to James Spada, the lovers did discuss marriage. "There was, of course, the not inconsequential problem of his existing wife, but at that point his relationship with Ardis was particularly acrimonious." As for the religious problems Grace would face with a non-Catholic divorced man, she was advised by her priest that things would work out fine if Holden took instruction and embraced the Catholic faith. This, she was assured, would make his previous marriage invalid.

Despite his widely stated desire to marry her, those close to him knew he had no intention of divorcing his wife. Several intimates quoted him saying, "If I were to lose Ardis, I would lose everything."

Grace Kelly's affair with William Holden apparently cured her of falling in love with married men. For compensation the heat generated by their mutual attraction in *The Country Girl* may well have been the key to winning her the Academy Award for best actress of 1954. In 1970 Holden and wife Ardis (aka the actress Brenda Marshall) divorced after twenty-nine years of marriage.

Brief Bio: Born William Franklin Beedle, Jr., April 17, 1918, in O'Fallon, Illinois, he was the product of a wealthy family in the chemical business. Attracted to acting, he appeared in student productions at the Pasadena Junior College in California, where a Paramount talent scout spotted him and signed him to a contract. Despite his classy good looks, his first film appearance was as an extra in a prison movie. In 1939, at the age of twenty-one, his first real screen role catapulted him to stardom. Cast as Joe Bonaparte, the ghetto youth who becomes a boxer and falls into the clutches of Adolphe Menjou and Barbara Stanwyck, Holden's box office appeal in *Golden Boy* led to a series of

The scene that was never in the movie. William Holden and Bing Crosby pose with Grace Kelly on the set of The Country Girl *in 1954. Both were in love with her in real life as well as in the film. But in the film itself, Holden never meets the glamorous Georgie character as shown here. This image of her is seen only in flashback.*

innocuous boy-next-door roles. Finally, after his World War II service as an army lieutenant, his handsome features weathered sufficiently at the age of thirty-two to win him two uniquely different roles in 1950, Gloria Swanson's writer/gigolo in *Sunset Boulevard* and Judy Holliday's intellectual idealist tutor in *Born Yesterday*. Three years later he got the Academy Award for best actor in *Stalag 17*.

Viewers of TV's movie channels have discovered many of his more than seventy-five films, among them *Rachel and the Stranger, Picnic, The Towering Inferno*, and the powerful *Network*.

Following his divorce, Holden had an on-again-off-again relationship with actress Stefanie Powers, twenty-four years his junior and best known for her TV role in "Hart to Hart." The two met in the anthropology department of a Los Angeles bookstore. Their shared interest led to frequent visits to his 1,216-acre Mount Kenya Safari Club in Africa and his home in Palm Springs, California. In 1981 he died alone in his Los Angeles apartment, the victim of a freak accident. He had fallen, hit his head, and lain comatose for a period of days until death overcame him. Because he was thought to be traveling, nobody wondered about his whereabouts until it was too late.

Although his death was headline news, there is no record of Princess Grace's reactions. So far as is known, she did not send a message of sympathy over the loss of a fellow actor, one she had loved and admired more than a quarter of a century before.

THE HOLLYWOOD "MONSTER MACHINE"

A short-lived 1955 fan magazine, *Hollywood Dream Girl*, contained this insightful comment: "In Hollywood, there is a monster machine that eats little girls alive, digests them and spits them out as movie stars, subdued and broken to its will. It has never been able to take so much as a nip out of Grace Kelly." In addition to Grace, issue number one of *Hollywood Dream Girl* contains rare photographs of Marilyn Monroe plus photographs taken *by* James Dean. It has become a collector's item.

HOLLYWOOD'S NEW GARBO?

According to celebrity journalist Bill Tusher writing in *Screen-land* magazine in 1955, that was the question the California film community was asking. Unlike other up-and-coming stars of the time, Grace Kelly had a built-in horror of the spotlight and a passion for privacy. As an example of her aversion to publicity stunts, *The Country Girl* producer William Perlberg admitted that Grace refused to do leg art. "It's all right for girls in that field but not for Grace. I don't remember Greta Garbo ever doing leg art!"

The Garbo tag popped up right after completion of *To Catch a Thief*. With the film finally in the can, Grace simply packed her bags and disappeared, declining to make herself available to the studio for photo layouts and interviews.

Referring to her cool aloofness and the aura of mystery surrounding her widely rumored love affairs, Tusher drew a convincing parallel with the fabled Garbo. "Like the immortal Sphinx of the Swedish wastes, Grace wants nothing more than to be alone!"

With good reason, Tusher pointed out. "Her early encounters with movieland gossip columnists succeeded only in reinforcing her determination to bolt the doors on her personal affairs.

"She was devastated by gossip items that fanned her friendship with Clark Gable and Ray Milland into romantic proportions and even cast her in the role of homewrecker when Milland was separated from his wife. She denounced these tidbits as slanderous untruths and inexcusable exaggerations."

A case can be made for a parallel with Garbo's retirement from the screen. Greta Garbo made her last movie in 1940, at the age of thirty-five, and disappeared into a self-styled retirement with no explanation but with teasing hints over the nearly five decades until her death that she might be tempted to make a comeback. Grace Kelly made her last feature film in 1956, at the age of twenty-six, and exchanged Grace Kelly the actress for the totally new persona Her Serene Highness Princess Grace of Monaco.

Despite her refusal to do cheesecake like other young stars, Grace did get talked into posing for this hokey "barefoot girl" still in 1953.

Unlike Garbo, she announced her decision to abandon her movie career and explained her reasons—at least to a point. Like Garbo, Grace Kelly the actress was an extremely complicated and private person whose reasons for abandoning her career at the height of her fame and power to marry a man she had met only twice before were so deeply embedded that she herself might not have understood them or been able to deal with them in any other way.

HOME FOR MONACO'S AGED

Always aware of her humanitarian responsibilities, Princess Grace was deeply troubled by the loneliness of elderly people spending their final years at Monaco's home for the aged. Some had been abandoned by their families. Many had no family at all. Grace organized volunteers to visit the home regularly. She joined them as often as possible.

HOOTING WITH LAUGHTER AT MOM'S OLD MOVIES

When Caroline, Albert, and Stephanie were children, one of their favorite pastimes was watching Grace Kelly films on their home screen. To tease their mom, they would make sarcastic remarks and hoot with laughter at her performances, especially the love scenes.

"THE HOT ICICLE"

One of the many nicknames Hollywood gagsters gave the unflappable Grace Kelly was "The Hot Icicle."

HOW A THANK-YOU NOTE CHANGED GRACE'S LIFE

A stickler for correct manners, Margaret Kelly taught her children how to behave properly in social circumstances. So it should have come as no surprise that Grace Kelly wrote Prince Rainier a charming thank-you note after her initial visit to his palace. The prince, also trained in the niceties, wrote back to say how glad he was that they had met. Soon a regular correspondence accelerated into a pen pal friendship of shared thoughts.

While the contents of these letters have only been hinted at, intimates have pointed out several of the things the two had in common and most likely felt comfortable discussing in writing if not face to face. Both had been lonely as children. Both were basically extremely shy among strangers. Both were practicing Catholics with a fundamental belief in their faith.

HOW GRACE'S PARENTS MET

In 1914 Jack Kelly and a group of his friends went swimming at Turner's Pool, a gathering place for young people in Philadelphia. At twenty-three, he was tall, handsome, and muscular from his daily labors as a bricklayer for his brother's contracting firm and his weekends perfecting his rowing skills on the Schuylkill River. Margaret Majer at sixteen was a classic beauty with blond hair, blue eyes, and the lithe figure of a natural athlete.

When Kelly first saw her she was standing near the diving board. Full of confidence, he introduced himself, listened attentively as she told him of her plans to study physical education at Temple University, and then asked her for a date.

She was busy, she said, and suggested he ask her out another time.

Nine years would go by—including Jack's overseas service in World War I—before they ultimately dated and then married in 1924.

HOW WOULD GRACE LIKE TO BE REMEMBERED?

According to Prince Rainier, Grace once told him she wanted to be remembered as "a decent human being and a caring one."

Princess Grace, who wanted to be remembered as "a decent human being and a caring one," will more likely be remembered for her beauty and her fairy-tale life. (Tom Hustler/Camera Press)

HOWARD HUGHES STRUCK OUT

Multimillionaire Howard Hughes's friendship with Cary Grant did not help him in his pursuit of Grace Kelly. Cary's wife in the early 1950s, Betsy Drake, recalled what happened when Hughes came to their house. Grace's technique for eluding Hughes was to use no makeup, screw her hair back in a bun, and wear her glasses. To the amusement of all, Howard Hughes was in the same room with Grace Kelly but failed to recognize her! As Drake said later, "Howard was on the make for every woman. He would make it a project. He went to such pains to get his various women—but he never got Grace!"

"I ALWAYS THOUGHT IT WOULD BE PEGGY"

Grace's father was the soul of tactlessness. While it was acknowledged in the Kelly family that his eldest daughter, Peggy, was his favorite, he made his preference clear to the world press after Grace won the Academy Award for *The Country Girl*. Interviewed by the press during the hubbub after the awards ceremony, he did not express pride in his middle daughter's accomplishments. Instead he said, "I always thought it would be Peggy. Anything Grace could do, Peggy could do better. How do you figure these things?"

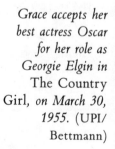

Grace accepts her best actress Oscar for her role as Georgie Elgin in The Country Girl, *on March 30, 1955.* (UPI/ Bettmann)

"I AM A BIT AFRAID OF MOVIE STARS"

In the autumn of 1955 noted journalist David Schoenbrun interviewed Prince Rainier as he prepared for a visit to America.
Amid rumors of a relationship with Grace Kelly, most of the
questions had to do with the bachelor prince's desire to marry.
As reported in *Collier's* magazine, Schoenbrun asked, "What are
the requisites for being a princess of Monaco? Can any girl be
your princess, a commoner, a movie star, a shop girl?"

Rainier responded, "I am free to marry the girl of my
choice, from any walk of life, from any nation. Whoever she is,
wherever she comes from, once we marry, she will be a Monégasque and she will be my princess. I can marry a parlormaid,
a shop girl—or a movie star, although of course I do not get to
meet many parlormaids or shop girls."

Anticipating that Schoenbrun's next question might be
about Grace Kelly, whom he had met only once the previous
spring, Rainier added, "Frankly, I'm a bit afraid of movie
stars."

"I CAN FOOL YOU, MOTHER. I CAN FOOL YOU ANYTIME"

This is an oft-repeated remark that Princess Caroline is supposed to have made to Princess Grace—but nobody has been
able to say when and where the immortal words were uttered.

"I HAVE DECIDED TO MARRY PRINCE RAINIER OF MONACO"

Grace Kelly chose the deck of New York's Staten Island ferry as
the place to tell Oleg Cassini that she was breaking their
engagement and why. "I have decided to marry Prince Rainier
of Monaco."

"I MUST BE THE BOSS . . ."

While still a bachelor in 1955 and before he proposed to Grace
Kelly, Prince Rainier candidly characterized his role as a pro-

spective husband. Interviewed by David Schoenbrun for *Collier's* magazine, he said, "I must be the boss, or else I'm not a man. At the same time, I'm not a dictator. It takes two to start a fight and two to make a marriage."

IDEAL HOUSEGUESTS

Princess Grace trained her children to be well-behaved houseguests. Her sister, Lizanne LeVine, was delightedly surprised when Caroline and Albert visited America as youngsters. As she told biographer James Spada, they made their own beds, straightened their rooms, pitched in with dinner and the dishes. "They were taught to do that, not to expect someone to wait on them all the time."

INITIAL PROBLEMS FOR STEPHANIE

After ending her two-year affair with Mario Oliver Jutard, Princess Stephanie underwent painful laser surgery to remove the tattoo of his initials from her behind.

INTERNATIONAL PATRON OF THE ARTS

Princess Grace actively supported a variety of international cultural activities. Among them were the rebuilding of London's Globe Theatre, the association La Sauvegarde de l'Art Français and the Union Internationale des Femmes Architectes in Paris, and the Irish-American Cultural Institute in New York and Dublin, of which she was international chair.

Ever aware of the plight of aging performers in motion pictures, she presided over numerous benefits in support of the American Motion Picture Relief Fund and also helped launch a home for retired film actors in France.

"IT'S ONLY QUININE WATER!"

In the early 1950s, when film stars were not supposed to be shown drinking or smoking, Grace Kelly was at a Hollywood cocktail party. As the photographers moved in to take their shots, a studio press agent rushed around removing highball glasses from the hands of the stars. Everyone cooperated except for Grace Kelly, who steadfastly refused to surrender her glass.

"It's only quinine water," she insisted.

"But Miss Kelly. People might think it's hard liquor."

Cool and unruffled, the determined young actress replied, "Let them think what they want. *I* know it's quinine water!"

JACK LACKED TACT (PART ONE)

In the fall of 1947 Grace Kelly excitedly told her parents she had been accepted by the American Academy of Dramatic Arts in New York. Her mother worried about the eighteen-year-old leaving home. All Jack Kelly said was "Let her go. She'll be back in a week."

JACK LACKED TACT (PART TWO)

Grace's parents traveled to New York from Philadelphia for the opening of her first Broadway play, *The Father*, starring Raymond Massey. Afterward, when they attended the cast party, Massey greeted Jack Kelly with surprise. "What on earth are you doing here, Kelly?"

"My daughter's in your play!"

Grace knew that Massey and her father knew each other because of a shared interest in rowing. But in a firm resolve to "make it" in show business on her own, she had purposely not mentioned who she was.

Massey was clearly delighted. "I had no idea you were her father!"

Jack Kelly abruptly changed the subject to Kell's recent winning of the Diamond Sculls in England. "Did you hear about my son's victory at the Henley Regatta?"

JACK LACKED TACT (PART THREE)

When Grace won her Academy Award for best actress in *The Country Girl*, her father was widely reported to have shaken his head in bewilderment and said, "I can't believe it. I simply can't believe Grace won. Of the four children, she's the last one I'd expected to support me in my old age."

"MRS. JACK" LACKED TACT

In a mother-of-the-bride-to-be newspaper series that appeared soon after her daughter's announced engagement, Margaret Kelly prattled on and on about Grace's "life and romances." With what she thought of as motherly pride she revealed, "Men began proposing to Grace when she was barely 15. Prince Rainer III was at least the 50th man!"

JEWEL THIEVES AT THE WEDDING (WHERE ARE YOU, CARY GRANT, WHEN WE NEED YOU?)

In his costarring role opposite Grace Kelly in *To Catch a Thief*, Cary Grant played a retired jewel thief who helped the authorities capture a cat burglar creating havoc on the Riviera.

Monaco could have used a real-life Cary Grant during the festivities surrounding the royal wedding. A Philadelphia friend of Jack Kelly's, Matthew H. McCloskey, and his wife had more than $50,000 worth of jewels stolen from their hotel suite. Bridesmaid Maree Pamp reported some $8,000 in jewels missing from her room, a loss that was exacerbated when she had to appear at various dress-up functions without her favorite adornments.

The biggest haul was five paintings valued at $95,000 stolen from the home of a Grimaldi family friend, Dr. S. Mikhailoff.

There has never been a report of the thieves being found or the property returned.

JENNIFER JONES SAYS "NO" TO GEORGIE

The original first choice to play Georgie Elgin in *The Country Girl*, Jennifer Jones had to cancel out of the film because she was pregnant. It was the plum role of 1954. Every big-name actress wanted it. The producer/director team of William Perlberg and George Seaton wanted Grace Kelly for the pivotal role opposite male leads Bing Crosby and William Holden. Despite Crosby's misgivings about Grace being too young and too pretty for the demanding and unglamorous role of his wife, Perlberg and Seaton prevailed, and Grace won an Oscar for best actress.

LOUIS JOURDAN

The quintessential continental lover in films, Jourdan was once described as being too handsome for his own good or the good of his career. He was ideal as Grace Kelly's tutor in her role as the sheltered Princess Alexandra in *The Swan*. While the Molnár story was by nature old-fashioned in its romanticism, the dormant passion Jourdan aroused in the "sleeping" princess was exquisitely touching and rewarding.

Brief Bio: Born Louis Gendre on June 19, 1919, in Marseilles, France. The son of a hotelman, he was educated in France, England, and Turkey and received his dramatic training at the Ecole Dramatique in Paris. He appeared in several French romantic films just as World War II was starting. When his father was arrested by the Gestapo, he and his brothers joined the Underground. After the war, film producer David O. Selznick cast him in *The Paradine Case* and the now-classic *Letter from an Unknown Woman* as the object of Joan Fontaine's unrequited desire. Other films include the rapturous *Gigi* with Leslie Caron and *The V.I.P.s*, in which he played a seedy playboy opposite Elizabeth Taylor.

"JUDYBIRD"

"Judybird" was Grace's affectionate nickname for her cherished friend Judith Balaban Quine. The two were beautiful, vivacious young women in April 1953 when they met at Judybird's wedding, which Grace attended because the groom was Jay Kanter, Grace's agent. Almost three years to the day later, in April 1956, Judy attended Grace's wedding as one of six bridesmaids.

In 1989 she wrote a bestselling memoir about the wedding and her enduring friendship, *The Bridesmaids: Grace Kelly and Six Intimate Friends.*

"JUST SHED A RESPECTFUL TEAR . . ."

Following Jack Kelly's death in 1960, the reading of his will gave a unique expression of his personal philosophy and feelings. After the expected preliminaries concerning executors and trustees, he wrote, "My family is raised and I am leaving enough so they can face life with a better than average start.

"As for me, just shed a respectful tear if you think I merit it, but I am sure you are all intelligent enough not to weep all over the place. I have watched a few emotional acts at graves, such as trying to jump into it, fainting etc., but the thoroughbred grieves in the heart.

". . . [L]ife owes me nothing. . . . I have known great sorrow and great joy. I had more than my share of success. . . . If I had the choice to give you worldly goods or character, I would give you character. The reason I say that is with character you will get worldly goods because character is loyalty, honesty, ability, sportsmanship and—I hope—a sense of humor." Public interest in his will in Philadelphia was so great, printed copies were put on sale for seven dollars.

AMY KANE

Grace Kelly's character in *High Noon* was Amy Kane, the young bride of the sheriff played by Gary Cooper. As a Quaker, she believed in nonviolence. Having turned in his badge, her new husband seemed as determined as she to start a new life until word reached town that four killers were coming to "get" him. Amy's desire for peace at any price ran counter to her husband's sense of moral obligation to confront the outlaws. What's more, she had her own moral dilemma to resolve when she had to choose between letting the man she loved be killed and using a gun to save his life.

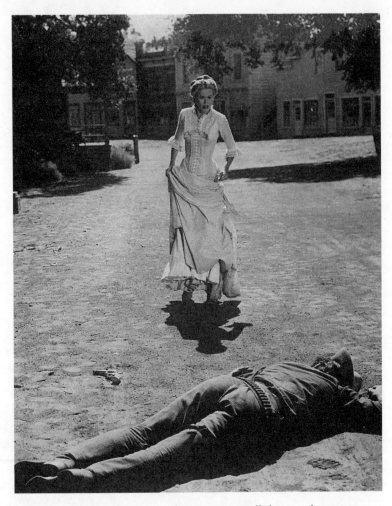

High drama in High Noon, *this is Grace Kelly's pivotal moment as Gary Cooper's Quaker bride, who must transcend her pacifist principles to save her husband's life.*

Grace Kelly was dissatisfied with her performance and felt she had much to learn about acting. The critics, however, agreed that she had held her own in at least one other memorable scene: the one in which she confronted the sheriff's discarded mistress, played by Mexican actress Katy Jurado.

THE KELLY BAG

Created by Hermès of Paris and named for Grace Kelly after it became a permanent part of her wardrobe, the Kelly Bag is a roomy, box-shaped bag distinguished by a narrow belt-style closing and tiny padlock. Long a fashion competitor of the reigning Chanel quilted classic with its heavy gold chains, the Kelly Bag of the 1990s is even more popular among fashionable women than when introduced more than thirty years ago. The price ranges from $2,000 to $10,000, depending on the materials, which include calfskin, ostrich, and lizard. There is a six-month waiting list for the Hermès original. Variations are more readily available from manufacturers and designers like Calvin Klein. A 1991 *New York Times* feature on busy women photographed at random on Manhattan streets showed a preponderance of the Kelly Bag.

THE KELLY KIDS AT PRAYER

As children Grace and her three siblings were taught a consecutive prayer by their mother. Kelly family biographer John McCallum relates how at mealtime, the four youngsters would recite individually, in descending order by age:

Peggy: Bless us, Lord, and these Thy gifts we are about to receive from Thy bounty through Christ our Lord.

Kell: Do unto others as you would have others do unto you.

Grace: Politeness is to do and say the kindest thing in the kindest way.

Lizanne: Amen.

GRACE KELLY COLD? NOT SO, SAYS JAMES STEWART

Interviewed a year after they costarred in *Rear Window*, James Stewart pooh-poohed the idea that Grace Kelly was aloof. As he told journalist Margaret Parton in a 1956 *Ladies' Home Journal* interview, "Grace, *cold*? Why, Grace is anything but cold. She

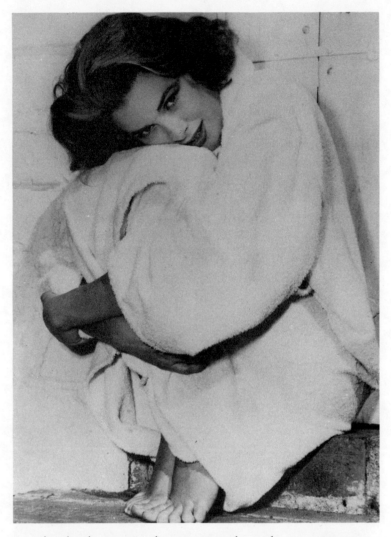

Grace's sultry beauty is evident even in such mundane situations as resting after a swim in the pool at her Hollywood home. (UPI/ Bettmann)

has those big warm eyes—and . . . well, if you ever have played a love scene with her, you know she's not cold. People who have inner confidence are not cold. Besides, Grace has that twinkle and a touch of larceny in her eye."

"GRACE KELLY: HOLLYWOOD'S NEWEST PROBLEM CHILD?"

This was the provocative blurb on the cover of *Screenland Magazine* for March 1955, a colorful example of Grace Kelly's growing superstar quality following the release of *To Catch a Thief*.

In typical fan magazine style of the time, the article called her "the girl who's the talk of moviedom" and chronicled her "femme fatale" romances with Ray Milland, Bing Crosby, Oleg Cassini, and Jean-Pierre Aumont. Despite the magazine's "shock" at her personal life, it concludes that she is "dedicated to her art rather than to her public and to Grace this is not snobbery but the secret of why she has the potential of greatness as an actress."

Grace Kelly publicity still sent out to the media by MGM in 1955.

GRACE KELLY IN BLACK NET HOSE?

It happened only once, early in her career. In a 1952 episode of the television series "Lights Out," Grace Kelly played a dance hall girl whose life was threatened. Her costume, reminiscent of the one worn by Marilyn Monroe in *Bus Stop*, featured black net hose, open-toed high-heeled shoes with red satin ribbons criss-crossed at her ankles, an extremely short red tulle skirt with huge chrysanthemums at the waist, a black satin strapless bodice, and a floating see-through kimono of patterned red lace.

"THE GRACE KELLY LOOK"

Designed for her by Oleg Cassini, who would later create "the Jackie look" for Jacqueline Kennedy, the wardrobe emphasized Grace's pale, delicate patrician looks. Among his designs was a formal gown in heavy taffeta, an almost antique soft pink chosen to complement her skin tones. It had a simple top and a complicated petallike skirt. When Milton Greene photographed her he also took some informal shots of her wearing one of Oleg's oversized sweaters.

When *Look* magazine ran the series, it put the sweater shot on the cover and the pink gown inside.

In 1954, Grace made America's Best Dressed list for the first time, wearing her Cassini "look."

GRACE KELLY (MADE-FOR-TV MOVIE)

Made with Princess Grace's blessings, this two-hour ABC-TV movie aired after her death, on February 21, 1983. Playing the title role was Cheryl Ladd, whose coloring and bone structure are remarkably like Grace Kelly's. Scrupulous attention to hairstyles, makeup, and wardrobe combined to enhance the viewer's sense of seeing Grace Kelly re-creating her own life. The story line followed her from her childhood in Philadelphia through her early days as an actress in New York and Hollywood stardom and ended with her courtship and marriage to Prince Rainier.

As fascinating as it is to watch Cheryl as Grace, it is equally intriguing to see how the famous people in her life have been portrayed. Lloyd Bridges and Diane Ladd played her parents, Jack and Margaret Kelly. Ian McShane was Prince Rainier, Alejandro Rey was Oleg Cassini. Rene Rousel was

Oleg Cassini clearly did not design this fringed number, a totally non–Grace Kelly "look." Whose design this was remains a minor mystery, as does Grace's agreeing to wear it.

Jean-Pierre Aumont, Van Corwith was William Holden, and Lomax Studdy was Alfred Hitchcock.

GRACE KELLY PAPER DOLLS

Noted illustrator Tom Tierney re-created more than thirty fashions worn by the actress/princess in major roles and events of her life in this charming paper-doll book (Dover Books, 1986). Sixteen full-color plates include three Grace dolls and one of Prince Rainier. Costumes, gowns, and outfits range from actress Grace Kelly's professional stage debut in 1949 to her costumes in *High Noon*, *Rear Window*, *To Catch a Thief*, and *The Swan* and on to her royal wedding gown and wardrobe highlights of her life as Princess Grace. The final ensemble is a Dior worn at a party in her honor a short time before her death.

"GRACE KELLY: THE AMERICAN PRINCESS"

"Grace Kelly: The American Princess" is a one-hour TV documentary produced in 1987 by Wombat Productions in association with Devillier Donegan Enterprises. Written and produced by Gene Feldman and Suzette Winter and directed by Feldman, it presents family, friends, and professional costars of Grace Kelly both before and after she married Prince Rainier, interspersed with clips from her films, newsreel footage, and archival stills.

Among those appearing are Rita Gam, Alec Guinness, Louis Jourdan, Katy Jurado, James Stewart, Stanley Kramer, Judith Balaban Quine, Grace's sister Lizanne LeVine, and Princess Grace herself. The narrator is Richard Kiley.

There are clips from such films as *High Noon*, *Mogambo*, *The Swan*, *To Catch a Thief*, *Dial M for Murder*, and *The Country Girl*; newsreel footage of Grace and Rainier's engagement, marriage, and their twenty-six years together before her death; and a retrospective of the Kelly family in stills and home movies.

This is a richly detailed, carefully documented biography that is worth watching again and again. It is frequently rerun on the Biography series on the Arts & Entertainment network and is also available in home video stores. For further details, contact Devillier Donegan Enterprises, 4401 Connecticut Ave., NW, Washington, DC 20008.

GRACE KELLY'S DOWRY ·

Among aristocratic European families, the bride's dowry was a tradition going back hundreds of years. Usually it involved an arranged marriage between families of comparable wealth and position. The transfer of land or money from the bride's family to the groom was in effect a business transaction enhancing the standing of each.

For much of Grace and Rainier's twenty-six year marriage, rumors would surface every so often about Jack Kelly having paid a two-million-dollar dowry, a figure vigorously refuted by family friend Jeffrey Robinson, who says he has seen the marriage contract in Rainier's private files: "I can categorically state that while certain financial arrangements were made, a two-million-dollar dowry was not involved."

GRACE KELLY'S WEDDING DRESS INSPIRES *FATHER OF THE BRIDE* DESIGNER

The satin-and-lace wedding gown worn by actress Kimberly Williams in the 1991 remake of *Father of the Bride* was inspired by Grace Kelly's real-life wedding gown. "I needed something that was beautiful, traditional, and young," said costume designer Susan Becker. "The closest thing was Grace Kelly's dress. I've always loved the way she looked at her wedding." Becker's bell-shaped creation with its long cathedral train was so heavy, a crew member was assigned to help Kimberly hold it up between takes. In contrast to Kelly's shoes, the younger actress walked down the aisle in white satin beaded running shoes.

JACK KELLY DURING WORLD WAR I

Grace's father served in France with the U.S. Army for over a year. Having joined up in 1917 as a private, he earned a field commission and was a lieutenant by the time he was discharged.

JACK KELLY STORMS THE OFFICES OF *CONFIDENTIAL*

In the early 1950s the forerunner of today's supermarket tabloids like the *National Enquirer* was a scandal sheet called *Confidential*. When it blew the whistle on Grace Kelly's affair with William Holden, Jack Kelly and son Kell stormed into the magazine's offices and roughed up the editors.

JACK KELLY'S "12-HOUR PASS"

During the festivities surrounding his daughter's wedding, Jack left the palace one night to play cards in a Philadelphia friend's hotel room. Mocking his royal son-in-law, he wisecracked, "I got out on a 12-hour pass but I want to be back on time so I won't get jugged for going AWOL."

JOHN HENRY KELLY

Grace Kelly's paternal grandfather, born in county Mayo, Ireland, in the 1840s, emigrated to America in the late 1860s at age twenty-two and married another Irish immigrant, Mary Costello, in 1869. By 1873 they were living in the Falls of Schuylkill in Philadelphia, where John worked in Dobson's Textile Mill. They had ten children, among them a daughter, Grace, who died at twenty-two on the verge of a promising acting career, and John Brendan, known as Jack, who would be Princess Grace's father.

"MA" KELLY'S CREDO

Grace Kelly's mother established a set of rules for her child: "Be just. Be punctual. Buy only what you need and pay cash." According to intimates, Grace tried to live by these rules all of her life.

MRS. KELLY ADMITS HER MISTAKE

Many years after Margaret Kelly's interference in her daughter's plans to marry Oleg Cassini, the designer was at a Philadelphia charity ball where he was to receive the Philadelphia Cup Award for his contributions to fashion. The presenter turned out to be Grace's mother. As she handed him the ceramic bowl, she whispered, "I think perhaps I made a mistake about you after all."

WALTER KELLY, "THE VIRGINIA JUDGE"

Grace Kelly's uncle Walter was an internationally famous performer in vaudeville, best known for his "Virginia Judge" monologue. A colorful, flamboyant man with the "gift for gab," he encouraged his niece in her theatrical ambitions as a child. He died in 1941, before he could see the fruits of his influence.

Described as "a wise and extraordinary man, a humorist of the first water and fine teller of stories," he is also known for the oft-repeated classic about the parish priest meeting Mary O'Toole on the street with something concealed under her arm. Asked what it was, the woman said, "Holy water, Father."

The priest took the cork out of the bottle and sniffed. "This is not holy water. It's whiskey."

"Glory to God," cried Mary, crossing herself. "Another miracle!"

THE KENNEDY ASSASSINATION: PRINCESS GRACE UNFAIRLY ATTACKED

On November 22, 1963, Princess Grace and her children were photographed at the opening of a carnival in Monte Carlo. One of the photographs of her holding an amusement-park rifle at the shooting gallery appeared the next day in the world press and was unfairly attacked for being "insensitive" to the murder of President Kennedy. The fact ignored by the press is that Monaco is seven hours ahead of Dallas, Texas. The picture of Grace and the rifle was taken nine hours before Kennedy's assassination.

JACK KENNEDY'S "NIGHT NURSE"

In 1954, when Jack Kennedy, then a U.S. senator, was hospitalized in New York City for back surgery, Jacqueline Kennedy tried to cheer him up by bringing her friend Grace Kelly to his hospital room late one night. "I'm the new night nurse," she whispered. The future president smiled but was too groggy from medication to enjoy the joke.

JOE KENNEDY DOUBLE-CROSSES OLEG CASSINI

Oleg Cassini thought he was close enough to Joseph P. Kennedy to ask his help in convincing Grace Kelly to marry him despite her family's objections. The year was 1955; the place was New York's elegant La Côte Basque restaurant. As an intimate of the Kennedy family, Oleg had designed clothes for Rose Kennedy and for her daughters, Pat and Eunice. He would later—in 1960—become First Lady Jacqueline Kennedy's official couturier, but for the moment his friendship with Joe Kennedy was such that they played golf regularly, dined together at exclusive clubs, and were known in sophisticated circles as men of the world.

When Cassini asked the older Kennedy's advice, Joe said, "Introduce me to the lucky girl and I'll settle everything. I guarantee it." As Cassini describes what happened next, "I arranged lunch at La Côte Basque. We sat at a corner table: Grace, demure and elegant as always; Joe Kennedy with his brilliant blue eyes, an incredibly vibrant man even then; and me. I was feeling pretty confident."

This confidence was short-lived. Joe Kennedy took Grace's hand and said, "Grace dear, the Kellys, the Kennedys, people like us, we have to stick together." To Cassini's chagrin, his friend did not then go on to say the Cassinis were also great.

Instead Kennedy said, "You know, Grace, I know this donkey. He's a pretty good boy, but you'd be making a terrible mistake to marry him!"

Cassini tried to save the situation by pretending that Kennedy had a bizarre sense of humor and was only kidding. The older man's motive quickly became clear when he began to stroke Grace Kelly's hand and suggested the two of them get together. "We have to discuss this thing, you and I," Kennedy told her. "You can count on me. I am at your total disposal."

A few years later, following Grace's marriage, Kennedy said, "Oleg, I probably did you a favor. Those Kellys would have been on you like octopuses. They would've driven you crazy."

Joe Kennedy's perfidy continued to haunt Oleg Cassini. There was every evidence that the Kennedy patriarch took perverse delight in bragging about the incident. After Jack Kennedy became president in 1960, Cassini became one of his White House intimates. The story about the "famous" lunch at La Côte Basque turned out to be one of JFK's favorites. More than once when the president's chums gathered informally, he would turn to Cassini and say, "Oleg, tell them how Dad screwed you up with Grace Kelly."

KINDERGARTEN AT THE ROYAL PALACE

When Caroline was four, her mother organized a kindergarten class within the confines of the palace for her daughter and other Monégasque girls of the same age. A year later, Albert and two little local boys joined the group.

KNITTING, EMBROIDERY, AND NEEDLEPOINT

Grace's mother began teaching her these basic skills at the age of eight. Sewing and cooking were also among the domestic skills Margaret Kelly insisted all her daughters perfect. Throughout her life Princess Grace was often seen knitting or doing needlepoint when she had a free moment.

On location in Colombia, South America, for Green Fire, *Grace Kelly as Catherine Knowland poses with unnamed horse.*

CATHERINE KNOWLAND

The name of Grace Kelly's character in *Green Fire* was Catherine Knowland, the owner of a coffee plantation in Colombia, South America. The potboiler plot revolved around a clash of wills between Catherine and mining engineer Stewart Granger, whose goal was to replace coffee beans with emerald mines. Bandits, mine cave-ins, and the exotic backcountry locations provided a colorful visual contrast to Catherine's glacial determination until Granger's "fiery" kisses melted her reserve. The final love scene was played in a torrential downpour with the soaking wet Catherine looking fabulous as she abandoned herself to passion.

STANLEY KRAMER SENDS A TELEGRAM

On August 10, 1951, film director Stanley Kramer sent the following telegram to Grace Kelly at the Elitch Gardens theater in Denver, where she was doing summer stock: Can you report Aug. 28, lead opposite Gary Cooper, tentative title High Noon.

LEADING MEN'S REACTIONS TO GRACE KELLY'S RETIREMENT

William Holden: "Women like Grace Kelly help us believe in the innate dignity of man and today that's what we desperately need."

Alec Guinness: "No matter where she lives, Grace will never lose her quality of spontaneity."

James Stewart: "She'll always have the class you find in a really great race horse."

Gary Cooper: "She's been a good actress and she deserves all the praise she gets."

Cary Grant: "It's a blow to our industry. If you know another Grace Kelly, will you send her out here?"

DR. JAMES LEHMAN

The Kelly family's personal physician, Dr. James Lehman, removed Princess Grace's appendix in April 1959 at the Clinic

Cecil in Switzerland. Rumors flew that she had cancer, that she was suffering from a series of miscarriages, and that she had a rare intestinal disease. At a press conference following surgery, Dr. Lehman assured everyone that the operation he performed was an appendectomy—and nothing more.

A year later, Dr. Lehman performed exploratory stomach surgery on Grace's father in Philadelphia. Jack Kelly had been ill for some time. The surgery revealed terminal cancer. He died on June 20, 1960, at the age of seventy.

SESTO LEQUIO

Monsieur Sesto Lequio was the retired truck driver who was the first person on the scene of the accident that killed Princess Grace and severely injured Princess Stephanie. According to leading British biographer Gwen Robyns, who interviewed him, the road to his house leads down from the exact place on the road from the Grimaldi farmhouse to Monaco where Grace's car plunged down the hillside.

Lequio, "a huge bear of a man," invited her into his house and told her, "I am tormented day and night wondering if I did enough to save the princess." He described how he dragged Princess Stephanie from the passenger side of the car and propped her against the wall like a broken doll. Because he could not extricate Princess Grace from the wreckage, he sprayed the car with a fire extinguisher to prevent leaking gasoline from exploding. He and a neighbor did all they could until the police and ambulance men removed the unconscious Princess Grace.

After saying good-bye to Lequio, Robyns returned to Monaco along the road where the accident occurred. Remembering the many times she had traveled the road with Princess Grace, she recalled, "I can still hear her say to me, 'One day there will be a terrible accident on that corner.' "

"A LESSON IN CATHOLIC MOTHERHOOD"

A tribute to Princess Grace by Terence Cardinal Cooke of New York praised her as "a lesson in Catholic motherhood."

THE LIBRARY BECOMES THE DELIVERY ROOM

For the birth of Princess Grace's first child, the library in the royal couple's private apartments in the palace was converted into a delivery room and draped in green silk in keeping with an old Irish superstition that green brings happiness and prosperity to the newborn.

LIFE'S QUANDARY

In April 1956, *Life* magazine found itself in a terrible quandary. Grace Kelly and Margaret Truman were getting married within two days of each other. Both had captured the American public's imagination and affection, Grace as the Oscar-winning actress who was ditching her career to become a princess, Margaret as President Harry Truman's only child and in that sense the princess from Missouri, who was hooking up with a top executive of the powerful *New York Times*.

Margaret's hometown wedding in Independence? Grace's international wingding in Monte Carlo? *Life* was sending reporters and photographers to both but the quandary was which blissfully wedded couple would appear on the cover.

Life was still a weekly magazine in 1956, each new issue impatiently awaited by its millions of readers. When the issue of April 30, 1956, hit the newsstands, its coverage of both weddings was colorful and in depth. But on the cover only one couple appeared: Margaret and Clifton Daniel in a beautiful portrait by photographer Arnold Newman.

This particular issue of *Life* has become a collector's item, not only because of the two weddings but also because it contains the first *Life* coverage of what the magazine headlined as "A Howling Hillbilly Success"—about Elvis Presley's "Heartbreak Hotel" reaching the top of the charts.

LIKE FATHER LIKE DAUGHTER

According to Prince Rainier himself, of his three children, the one who most resembles him is Princess Caroline. He described his older daughter as outspoken, quick-tempered, and "more Mediterranean" in temperament than Prince Albert, who resembles his mother physically and also has the tranquil personality she had.

ABE LINCOLN'S FIRST LOVE

In 1950, Grace Kelly appeared in the television drama "Ann Rutledge" based on the early life of Abraham Lincoln as a circuit rider and lawyer in Illinois. It was produced by one of the pioneers of long-form television dramas, Fred Coe. Aged twenty, Grace played the future president's first love, the beautiful, ethereal, but doomed Ann Rutledge, who died before she and Abe were to marry.

LIZ WEARS THE KRUPP DIAMOND AT GRACE'S FORTIETH BIRTHDAY BASH

The first time Elizabeth Taylor wore her newly acquired Krupp diamond in public was at Princess Grace's fortieth birthday party in Monaco. A gift from husband Richard Burton, the flawless 33.19-carat stone had once belonged to Vera Krupp, the wife of German munitions tycoon Alfred Krupp, and was said to have cost Burton more than $300,000.

According to Elizabeth, the gift was the result of a Ping-Pong match. Richard, an excellent player, challenged her to a match, promising to buy her a perfect gem if she could score ten points against him. "He was so cocky I got him sloshed and beat him!"

The Krupp diamond dazzled Grace's guests. The size of a peach pit, it became one of Elizabeth's favorite jewels, worn not only for formal occasions but also just for hanging around. Visitors to Taylor's home have described seeing it casually left on her bathroom sink like a piece of costume jewelry.

Once, in discussing the diamond, she remarked on the strange coincidence that the precious gem once owned by a Nazi munitions tycoon should end up on the finger of "a little Jewish girl like me."

Three years after Grace's fortieth birthday, Liz returned the compliment by inviting the Grimaldis to her own fortieth celebration in Budapest, where she had each hotel suite redecorated to reflect the personality of each guest. Taylor's order to her decorator? "Make it pretty enough for a princess!"

LIZANNE NAMES HER FIRST CHILD GRACE

Less than a year after marrying Donald LeVine, Lizanne had her first child in May 1956. She named the baby girl for her sister; Grace LeVine was christened in St. Madeline's Church in Germantown.

GENE LONDON

Fashion historian Gene London has amassed America's largest private collection of period costumes. Among more than sixty thousand items of wearing apparel and accessories are two original gowns worn by Grace Kelly in two separate films. One is the lavish gold lamé ball gown trimmed with golden doves that Edith Head designed for the memorable masquerade scene in *To Catch a Thief*. The other is the breathtakingly romantic Helen Rose summer gown of cream chiffon and lace festooned with pearls that perfectly expressed Grace Kelly's tender torment as the lovelorn Princess Alexandra in *The Swan*.

London's passion for collecting began during his twenty years as producer/director and star of the award-winning children's television show "The Gene London Show" in Philadelphia. The local CBS costume department knew of his interest in vintage fashion and was often able to provide rare items for the delight of audiences. Celebrity guests were intrigued by his enthusiasm and also sent him items, but what made him a full-time collector and exhibitor was the generosity of Joan Crawford. Despite her "mean" reputation, Crawford was outgoing in praise of things she liked. One day she wrote a "fan" letter to Gene London, complimenting him on his TV show. Having just bought a "Joan Crawford" dress at a thrift shop, he sent it to her for authentication. "Sorry," the star said, the dress was a fake. To make up for it, she sent him a three-piece chiffon jumpsuit and, as the friendship ripened, an enormous box of her personal belongings.

It was then that Gene London decided to devote his full-

Gene London with model
wearing the Edith Head
gown Grace Kelly wore in
To Catch a Thief.
(Photo courtesy Gene
London)

time efforts to housing and expanding his collection in a vast
ten-thousand-square-foot studio in New York City. Among his
treasures are clothes designed by Adrian, Edith Head, and
Travis Banton and authenticated garments worn by Greta
Garbo, Jean Harlow, Marlene Dietrich, Marilyn Monroe, Humphrey Bogart, Errol Flynn, and others. His Hollywood on
Parade exhibition is continually on tour nationwide at museums,
shopping malls, and special cultural events.

"Among the most popular items in my collection," says

London, "are the two Grace Kelly gowns. Perhaps it's because her film career was so short and her life as a princess came to such a sudden and tragic end. But when her gowns are displayed you can feel the special emotion they generate."

For information about Gene London's collection and exhibitions, contact Gene London, The Gene London Studios, 897 Broadway, New York, NY 10003; (212) 533-4105.

TRACY LORD

The name of Grace Kelly's character in *High Society* was Tracy Lord. The film was a musical remake of *The Philadelphia Story* by Philip Barry, who created the role of Tracy Lord for Katharine Hepburn. In some respects Grace was at a decided no-win disadvantage stepping into Hepburn's shoes. Hepburn's finely tuned eccentric was a flamboyant American original. In essence Kelly was simply too "soft" to convey the haughty hard-edged superiority of Barry's heroine. For fans of Hepburn's Tracy Lord, Kelly's portrayal was at times a faint echo of Hepburn's accent and cadences.

Comparisons aside, Grace Kelly looked glorious and in this her final film had the rare opportunity to play opposite Bing Crosby and Frank Sinatra and to be surrounded by the music of Cole Porter and the wit of trumpeter Louis Armstrong.

Grace Kelly filmed *High Society* just before leaving Hollywood to marry Prince Rainier. Her gaiety and high expectations for the future gave her Tracy Lord a warmth and tenderness that she was supposed to be lacking until the film's lovey-dovey conclusion. The big hit song from *High Society* was "True Love," which she sang in a romantic duet with Bing Crosby in the film and which became the theme of her engagement to Prince Rainier. In the weeks before their wedding, their arrival at a nightclub or a ball was always greeted by the band playing "True Love."

"LORD OF THE ROCK AND SEA"

This is one of the more colorful designations accorded Prince Rainier by his courtiers in the early years of his reign. The "rock" meant the royal palace built on the big promontory overlooking "the sea," i.e., the Mediterranean.

LOVER AND PRESENTER

At the 1955 Academy Award ceremonies few film fans knew that the actor who presented Grace Kelly with her Oscar for best actress in *The Country Girl* was also her lover. He was costar William Holden.

LUNCH WITH THE IN-LAWS

Bride-to-be Grace Kelly's first social engagement on the day of her arrival in Monaco in April 1956 was a small family luncheon. Among those present were Rainier's father, Count Pierre de Polignac, whom she had met in California; his mother, Princess Charlotte; his stepmother, Princess Ghislaine; and his sister, Princess Antoinette.

GENE LYONS

Actor Gene Lyons was the first man Grace Kelly seriously considered marrying. Tall, handsome, sensitive, and somewhat shy, the red-haired actor came from an Irish ancestry similar to hers but with one critical difference. The Kelly immigrants had become rich and powerful. The Lyons immigrants had remained poor.

The two met at the Elitch Gardens summer theater in Denver in 1951. By the time they had returned to New York for further study and to try their luck in TV drama, they were deeply in love—"besotted with each other," friends recalled—and talking of marriage.

Lyons was the first of a small legion of would-be husbands whom Grace took home to Philadelphia to meet her family. And he was the first to undergo the ruthless scrutiny of Grace's parents. Margaret Kelly, for instance, investigated the young actor's past and discovered he had been married and was seeking an annulment. Although his brooding looks were compared to Brando, Gene was well on his way to being an alcoholic. It

William Holden presented Grace Kelly with her Academy Award for best actress in The Country Girl.

was a portent of the emotional instability that would keep him from realizing his true potential as an actor.

Grace continued to see him while also dating others. As

her career began to take off, his remained static. Ultimately her life in the fast lane of increasing film success left him in a state of misery, drinking more and more. Despite her frequent absences on location, Lyons believed she was faithful to him and that they were a couple. When Grace finally broke up with him and took up with Jean-Pierre Aumont, Lyons was inconsolable. His drinking accelerated to the point of almost obliterating his original charismatic appeal. The discipline and demands of the theater and films were soon beyond his powers of concentration.

Still mindful of his feelings, Grace sent a telegram to Gene telling him about her engagement to Prince Rainier before it was officially announced. The news and his addiction nearly destroyed him in the mid-1950s, but he was able to pull himself together to appear in a supporting role on the TV series "Ironside" with Raymond Burr. After the series ended in 1975, he had reached the end of his rope and died a short time later.

"A MAIDEN SCHOOLTEACHER"

Oleg Cassini's first date with Grace Kelly in 1953 was for lunch at the famed Colony restaurant in New York City. She wore a severely tailored suit and glasses, a look he described as "a great beauty trying to pass as a maiden schoolteacher."

His challenge? "To defrost her."

MAKING GRACE JEALOUS

In 1954, at the height of her romance with Oleg Cassini, Grace went on location in the jungles of Colombia for *Green Fire.* Cassini had wanted to accompany her. When she refused, he set out to make her jealous by holding a lavish birthday party for Italian film star Pier Angeli, inviting four hundred guests to his Manhattan home. Grace's reaction? "I see you are keeping yourself busy."

MAMOU

This was Caroline, Albert, and Stephanie's affectionate nickname for their paternal grandmother, Princess Charlotte.

A MAN WHO WOULD NOT BECOME "MR. KELLY"

At the time of her twentieth wedding anniversary in 1976, Princess Grace told her old friend journalist Curtis Bill Pepper about her problems as a single woman who was also an internationally famous movie star. "I was a star, but I wasn't happy. My life was empty. I wanted to marry, but it had to be someone who wouldn't become Mr. Kelly."

THE *MARNIE* ANNOUNCEMENT

On March 20, 1962, Alfred Hitchcock announced that Princess Grace would come out of retirement to play the title role in *Marnie*. His public comments about her "sex appeal . . . the finest in the world" outraged the Monégasques to the point that she withdrew from the negotiations. The role was subsequently played by Tippi Hedren.

JACK MARSHALL

New York writer Jack Marshall was helping to cast a Broadway show in 1950 when Grace Kelly showed up at his tiny Times Square office. The play was *Josephine* by Sally Benson, whose future credits would include *Junior Miss*, *Shadow of a Doubt*, and *Meet Me in St. Louis*. A then unknown young actor, Leslie Nielsen, had been signed for the male lead as a Canadian Air Force pilot. The role Grace Kelly hoped to get was the love interest opposite him.

Until now, Marshall has never talked to a reporter about his love affair with Grace Kelly for one simple reason. "Nobody asked. It's hard to believe it was over forty years ago. I remember and cherish every moment of our time together."

Her prim determination was a sharp contrast to the other young hopefuls of the period. Wearing her trademark white gloves, she introduced herself with formality and, without trying to make small talk, immediately opened her portfolio of credits. "They were all modeling jobs. Her acting credits were zilch. Her voice was shy and whispery; no projection for the theater. But what hit me like a sledgehammer was her face! The most beautiful face I've ever seen, a madonnalike saintly face. Even now I choke up when I think about her."

Marshall arranged for the audition. She was exquisite on the stage, but as he feared, her voice didn't project. The role was given to another young actress, Betsy Von Furstenburg. The play, unfortunately, never opened, but Jack Marshall's friendship with Grace Kelly ripened into a lyrical if brief love affair. "I can't speak for her, of course, but for me it was serious. She was living at the Barbizon Hotel for Women at the time. We were like other young lovers in our early twenties, hanging out at jazz clubs like the Three Deuces to hear Charlie Ventura or the Hickory House to see Marian McPartland. There was an air of innocent possibility in the New York of the early 1950s, and we were part of it."

Small details create a larger mosaic. He remembers her skin was as smooth and pale as alabaster and was never affected by the large quantities of junk food she ate, her number-one favorite being frozen Milky Ways. Her spiritual needs were met by frequent quiet visits to stately St. Patrick's Cathedral on Fifth Avenue as well as the more modest St. Agnes Church on a quiet side street near Grand Central Station.

Although marriage was never discussed, Marshall clung to the possibility of a long-term relationship. Once Grace landed her first film role in *Fourteen Hours* and her subsequent role in *High Noon*, he had to face the fact that her career was her top priority. She stayed in touch with him long after they stopped seeing each other. "She was a great letter writer. She would scribble little personal notes on heavy bond paper with her monogram at the top. GK! In fact my nickname for her was Geekay—based on the monogram."

On her subsequent trips to New York, Marshall escorted her to various events, but gradually it became clear that her burgeoning career left little if any room for him. Conceding that he could have written to her in Monaco after her marriage to Prince Rainier and perhaps been invited to visit the palace, Marshall chose to respect the privacy of their "brief moment" in a separate compartment of his life.

Asked if he could pinpoint one memorable aspect of her character, Marshall pondered thoughtfully for a moment before replying, "She spoke kindly of people who were unkind to her."

GROUCHO MARX CONSOLES JUDY GARLAND

When Judy Garland lost the best actress Academy Award to Grace Kelly in 1955, Groucho Marx sent her a telegram: Dear Judy: This is the biggest robbery since Brinks. Groucho Marx.

MAUGHAM AT THE WEDDING

W. Somerset Maugham, the renowned British author of such classics as "Rain," *Of Human Bondage*, and *The Razor's Edge* and a longtime resident of the Côte d'Azur, was among those invited to the wedding of Grace and Rainier. The wedding turned out to be "no fun" according to Maugham biographer Ted Morgan. Maugham had to get into full evening dress at eight in the morning and sit for three hours in an icebox of a cathedral. "But the lunch that followed at the palace was worth it, with tubs of caviar, mountains of foie gras and oceans of champagne."

His wedding gift to the newlyweds was a three-volume collection of his short stories bound in leather. The only television interview he gave during the wedding festivities was with Arlene Francis for NBC-TV. It was arranged by Jeannie Sakol, coauthor of this book.

ELSA MAXWELL'S POOL PARTY

International party giver Elsa Maxwell gave a costume ball to celebrate the opening of an indoor swimming pool at the Hôtel de Paris in Monte Carlo in 1959. Grace and Rainier loved dressing up. For this event the prince wore a bald wig and fierce mustache, while his beautiful consort disguised herself in a rubber face mask with fat cheeks and braids and a floppy straw hat. When the other guests jumped into the new pool as part of the celebration, the Grimaldis joined them.

VERA MAXWELL BLAMED STEPHANIE

All evidence and witnesses to the contrary, Princess Grace's friend of twenty years and fashion designer Vera Maxwell was openly persistent in expressing her belief that Princess Stephanie was driving the car the day of the fatal accident. Six years after the tragedy she was quoted in the June 1988 issue of *Good Housekeeping* magazine as saying "Stephanie—as everybody knows—was the cause of her mother's death. She was a novice driver. Her mother let her drive an old gearshift car; they came across from a tiny country road to a main highway, and the child did not know how to shift gears properly. They went down a ravine and hit a tree."

Having said her piece in the strongest possible terms, Maxwell then added, "I think Rainier was quite right to put it out that Grace had an embolism, and it was not Stephanie's fault."

Vera Maxwell has stood painfully alone with her convictions. In addition to the medical evidence and the eyewitness accounts of those on the accident scene, there is the matter of Princess Grace's standard of ethics. Challenging Maxwell in *Good Housekeeping*, Grace's cousin Christian de Massy said, "Not for one minute would Grace have let Stephanie drive. No way would she have done anything illegal. She would never drive into Monaco and have the police saluting when Stephanie didn't have a license."

VIRGINIA MCKENNA TURNED IT DOWN

Because British film star Virginia McKenna turned down the role of Linda Nordley in *Mogambo*, Grace Kelly was tested and signed in 1952. Over a decade later, McKenna went to Africa on a different project, *Born Free*, in which she costarred with her husband, Bill Travers—and Elsa the lioness.

MEETING JEAN-PIERRE AUMONT WAS "FOR THE BIRDS"

In the summer of 1953 Grace Kelly and Jean-Pierre Aumont met as costars in a television biography of the celebrated American ornithologist John James Audubon, whose nineteenth-century paintings of America's birds have become part of the nation's heritage. Ten years older than Grace, the debonair French actor had only recently recovered from the accidental death of his wife, actress Maria Montez, who had drowned after collapsing in her bathtub.

Their "friendly" romance ended when the project ended, each leaving to fulfill other commitments. But they would meet again two years later on the French Riviera, where they fell "seriously" in love. The affair seemed to be leading to marriage, but by a twist of fate Grace was asked to have her photograph taken with Prince Rainier at his palace in Monaco.

"AUNT" FLOSSIE MERCKEL

A close friend and bridesmaid for Margaret Kelly, "Aunt" Flossie became Ma Kelly's right-hand social secretary and bookkeeper, chauffeuring Grace and Lizanne to dancing classes and generally acting as surrogate mother when needed.

RAY MILLAND

He was forty-nine when the twenty-three-year-old Grace Kelly costarred with him in Alfred Hitchcock's *Dial M for Murder*. The distinguished and much-admired actor had won an Academy Award in 1945 for his breakthrough performance as an alcoholic in *The Lost Weekend*. Married since 1932, his many romances were endured by his wife, Mal—until he fell head over heels in love with Grace in 1953. The two lovers did little to hide their affair. As biographer James Spada wrote, "Gossip

He broke her heart twice, once as her murderous husband in Dial M
for Murder, *the other, more devastating time as her real-life lover who
refused to divorce his wife for her. Ray Milland and Grace Kelly.*

in Hollywood spreads faster than Southern California fires
whipped by hot Santa Ana winds." The "heat" was so intense
that Mal could no longer pretend indifference. The Millands
separated. Ray took an apartment in Hollywood, where he and
Grace all but officially lived together.

When the Hollywood establishment turned viciously

against her, Grace was naively unprepared. Being in love and wanting to marry the man she loved seemed to her to be all that mattered. The veiled whispers and muted hints in the gossip columns led to an all-out attack in a scandal magazine, *Confidential*, that said the whole town was laughing over suave Ray Milland leaving his wife and children and going "ga-ga over Grace."

In practical terms their relationship threatened to undermine Grace's budding career as well as Ray's lifestyle. As a friend reminded him, most of his assets were in his wife's name, and if ever there were a publicly "guilty party," it was he. His desertion of home and family could have left him both penniless and potentially unemployable.

According to Grace's sister Lizanne, Grace was seriously committed to Ray and was heartbroken when the affair ended and he returned to his wife and family. Of some consolation was a phone call from Alfred Hitchcock offering a starring role opposite James Stewart in *Rear Window*. At the same time, Milland's next role cast him opposite newcomer Joan Collins in *The Girl in the Red Velvet Swing*, the story of an older man obsessed with a younger woman!

Brief Bio: Reginald Truscott-Jones was born on January 3, 1905, in Neath, Wales. After three years as a Royal Guards officer, he debuted in British films in 1929 using the name Spike Milland, a variation on his stepfather's surname, Mullane. Changing again to Raymond Milland, he struck out for Hollywood in 1930. Handsome, charming, and debonair, he appeared in more than seventy-five films before *The Lost Weekend* in 1945 and nearly another fifty thereafter, costarring with actresses ranging from Marlene Dietrich and Paulette Goddard to Ann Todd and Marjorie Reynolds. As he grew older, he chose to appear without the usual hairpiece affected by balding male stars. Among his best character roles was that of Oliver's unyielding father in *Love Story* and its sequel. A respected director of TV movies, he also starred in the 1959–60 TV series "Markham." When Princess Grace died, an enterprising reporter called the seventy-seven-year-old actor for a statement, but he was too upset to come to the phone. He died nearly four years later, on March 10, 1986, in Torrance, California.

A MINK STOLE

With her earnings from her first film, *Fourteen Hours*, Grace Kelly bought herself a mink stole, which was considered the height of fashion sophistication in the early 1950s.

MISTRAL THE CAT

In Paris in 1976, the eleven-year-old Princess Stephanie found a black-and-white alley cat, which she adopted and named Mistral, French for "north wind." Because Prince Rainier adamantly refused to allow cats inside the Grimaldis' Paris home, the little princess had to keep her pet in exile in the garden.

MOLESTED BY AL CAPP

Al Capp, creator of the cartoon series "L'il Abner," auditioned Grace Kelly for the role of Daisy Mae in the Broadway musical based on his Dogpatch characters. When she arrived at his office, he was alone and took advantage of the situation to sexually molest her. She fought him off and managed to escape in tears with her dress torn. Although tempted to bring charges against him, she decided it would reflect badly on her own reputation.

As it turned out, she was not his only victim. As reported by James Spada in his biography of Grace Kelly, Al Capp was arrested in April 1971 and charged with adultery, sodomy, and indecent exposure after inviting a married college student to his room following a lecture he had delivered. Nearly a year later, in February 1972, Capp plea-bargained to have two of the three charges dropped, pleaded guilty to attempted adultery, and was fined five hundred dollars plus court costs.

MONACO, NOT MOROCCO

In 1955 Americans knew about Monte Carlo, but few had ever heard of Monaco, much less how to pronounce it (Mohn-ah-co). Margaret Kelly was among those who at first thought her

The coat of arms of the rulers of Monaco. (Photo courtesy of the Monaco Board of Tourism.)

daughter wanted to marry the prince of Morocco and couldn't understand why!

MONACO TOURISM

If you're planning to visit Monaco, for up-to-date information on hotels, restaurants, current events, and places pertaining to the life and good works of Princess Grace, write to Monaco Government Tourist and Convention Bureau, 845 Third Ave., New York, NY 10022; (212) 759-5227; or Direction du Tourism de Monaco, 2 a Blvd des Moulins, Monte Carlo, MC 98030 Monaco; 93 30 87 01/93 50 60 88; fax (33) 93 50 92 80.

MONACO TRADITION: ANNUAL EVENTS

The Feast of Sainte-Dévote, Patron Saint of Monaco: On January 27, the relics of the fourth-century martyr are carried in procession from the cathedral to the Church of Sainte-Dévote. As part of the proceedings, the sea is blessed and a small boat is burned.

The Saint Martin Gardens Ball: On August 8, a ball in honor of a sixteenth-century cult of Saint Roman is held in the Saint Martin Gardens in Monte Carlo.

The Bonfires of Saint John: On June 23–24, folk songs and dances around a bonfire are held at the place du Palais and the place des Moulins in Monte Carlo.

The Monte Carlo International Circus Festival: In February the

A panoramic view of Monte Carlo. (Photo courtesy of the Monaco Board of Tourism.)

world's top circus acts join together to put on a show of unparalleled splendor.

The Monte Carlo International Fireworks Festival: In July and August the night sky of Monaco explodes in dazzling color illuminations similar to the fireworks in the love scene between Grace Kelly and Cary Grant in the film *To Catch a Thief.*

The Monte Carlo International Tennis Championships: Around Easter, this tournament at the Monte Carlo Country Club and Monaco Tennis Club attracts celebrity and tournament players from around the world.

The Monaco Grand Prix: In May the world's premier auto racing event roars through the winding streets of Monaco.

MONACO'S HOSPITAL

One of her first projects as Princess Grace was Monaco's grim old hospital. The rooms were so drab and depressing she couldn't see how any patient could recover in such surroundings. Despite resistance from the entrenched hospital staff, she brightened the hospital with cheerful colors, paintings on the walls, and fresh flowers.

In 1958, two years after her marriage, the hospital was renamed the Princess Grace Hospital, where sadly she was to die twenty-four years later.

THE MONEGASQUE MADONNA

The rock-and-roll press called Princess Stephanie the Monégasque Madonna after the release of her first album and the accompanying sexually intensive promotion campaign. The "Madonna" reference of course was directed at the American rock star and not at the biblical image of sainted motherhood.

MONOIKOS

The sixth-century B.C. name for the promontory overlooking the Mediterranean where Monaco stands today was Monoikos.

"MONTE CARLO . . . C'EST LA ROSE"

An ABC-TV special about Monaco hosted by Her Serene Highness, Princess Grace, in 1968 was entitled "Monte Carlo . . . C'est la Rose." Produced by veteran documentarian David Wolper, it shows Grace in various areas of the principality introducing such performers as French singer Gilbert Becaud, French actress Françoise Hardy, and British comedian Terry-Thomas in separate musical vignettes.

"I play Ed Sullivan" is how Grace described her role.

MONTE CARLO GAMBLERS BET ON THE ROYAL BABY'S SEX

In the weeks before the birth of Grace and Rainier's first child, gamblers at the Monte Carlo casino were laying five to seven odds that the baby would be a boy. (It was, of course, a girl, Caroline.)

MORNING SICKNESS ALL DAY LONG

Princess Grace's first pregnancy was physically trying almost from the moment of conception. She felt nauseated for months, later confiding to reporter Olga Curtis, "They told me about morning sickness, but they didn't tell me you could be sick all day every day."

Her childhood tendency to colds returned with a vengeance. She suffered sore throats and viruses throughout the entire nine months before the birth of Princess Caroline.

"THE MOST COOPERATIVE ACTRESS I EVER DIRECTED"

This was Alfred Hitchcock's description of Grace Kelly.

On location in South America for Green Fire, *Grace holds a gourd given to her by locals.*

MOTHER BITES CHILD

By the early 1960s Princess Caroline was at the hellcat stage
and difficult to control. One of her naughtier habits was biting

Princess Grace was portrayed as a worried mother in a People *cover
story for September 1, 1975, when Stephanie, ten, Albert, seventeen,
and Caroline, eighteen, were at various stages of rebellion. (From*
People. People Weekly is a registered trademark of the Time Inc.
Magazine Company, used with permission.)

her little brother, Albert. Grace did everything she could think of to stop her daughter's attacks. Warnings, reason, and punishment didn't help. Little Albert did nothing to defend himself either. Finally Her Serene Highness bit Caroline's arm hard enough to show her how it felt.

Caroline stopped biting her brother.

"MY LORD PRINCE, I CONGRATULATE YOU ON YOUR SON AND HEIR"

On March 14, 1958, a mere fourteen months after the birth of Caroline, Princess Grace gave her husband and the people of Monaco what they had so long desired, a male heir to the throne. Prince Albert Alexandre Louis Pierre weighed eight pounds, eleven ounces. He was born in the palace as his sister before him had been. When Dr. Emile Hervet, the royal obstetrician, stepped out of the delivery room to where Prince Rainier awaited, he said, "My Lord Prince, I congratulate you on your son and heir."

When Rainier announced the birth on Radio Monte Carlo, his voice shook with emotion. "Monégasques and residents of the principality, you will understand my emotion and very great joy in announcing to you that the princess, my beloved wife, has given birth to a little prince. Let us thank God for this new happiness, this proof of His special blessing."

NASTY NEWSCASTER

In the early 1950s Edward P. Morgan of the American Broadcasting Company was known as a "distinguished newscaster." When Grace Kelly and Prince Rainier invited President Eisenhower to their April 1956 wedding, Morgan turned nasty and condescending. Reporting from the White House, Morgan sneered, "President Eisenhower in all probability will designate a personal ambassador to represent him. I'd kind of like to suggest that Mr. Eisenhower designate Walt Disney. In one gracious gesture that would confirm what so many people suspect, that we Americans—the public in general and the administration in particular—prefer fairytales to the stark non-fiction of everyday life."

One can only speculate on the reason for this mean-spirited outburst. Was it indigestion? Jealousy of Prince Rainier? Or a spoiler's compulsion to throw rocks at the general public's pleasure in the romance?

NEVER IN VOGUE

As a photographer's model, Grace Kelly appeared on the covers of *Redbook*, *Cosmopolitan* (pre–Helen Gurley Brown), and the

Grace Kelly "fashion" pose from MGM. The peasant blouse trimmed with lace and enormous striped taffeta skirt are emblematic of early 1950s style.

Ladies' Home Journal in 1950 but was not chic enough for the high-fashion image of *Vogue*.

"NEVER MUCH OF A DRINKER"

In her autobiography Ava Gardner recalls an impromptu champagne party on the *Mogambo* location in Africa. Grace, she says, "was a great lady and also great fun, but she was never much of a drinker, though she tried hard. Her little nose would get pink, she'd get sick and we'd have to rescue her."

NEW YORK FILM CRITICS CIRCLE AWARD

In 1955 the New York Film Critics called Grace Kelly's acting in *The Country Girl* "the outstanding performance of 1954." Usually this prestigious award is the forerunner of the Oscar, and in Grace's case it was so when she got the best actress Academy Award for her role as Bing Crosby's tormented wife.

NIGHTGOWNS AND HITCHCOCK

On two separate occasions Grace defied Alfred Hitchcock and prevailed. In *Dial M for Murder*, he wanted her to wear a plush velvet robe when she answers the telephone for the murder scene at the desk. Grace's objection was based on the fact that a sleeping woman is going to answer a ringing phone just as she is when she awakens—in her nightgown. Hitchcock considered and agreed. In *Rear Window* he demanded her sheer nightgown be augmented with falsies. Grace was humiliated. Designer Edith Head made some clever tucks instead, to which the director enthused, "See what a difference it makes?"

A NINE-MAN CREW PLUS ONE POODLE

When the Rainiers' honeymoon yacht, the *Deo Juvante II*, set sail from Monte Carlo harbor, its crew consisted of nine men plus Grace's black poodle, Oliver.

"NO HURRY TO MARRY"

As reported on October 1, 1991, in the international edition of the *Herald Tribune*, Prince Albert, one of the world's most eligible bachelors, said he was in no hurry to get married. The thirty-three-year-old heir apparent to Prince Rainier's throne told Reuters News, "Of course I want to get married eventually and have children. But it's not for other people to decide when the time is right. It's my life after all."

NO KENNEDY ENGAGEMENT FOR STEPHANIE

Supermarket tabloids to the contrary, Princess Stephanie has not only never planned to marry John Kennedy, Jr., but they also have never even met.

NO STATISTICS, THANK YOU

Apart from her date of birth, November 12, 1929, Grace Kelly adamantly refused to divulge such personal statistics as bust, weight, and hip measurements. Other young actresses of the 1950s gave out such intimate information as part of the publicity build-up. Grace's attitude? "It's nobody's business."

NO UNDERWEAR

During her brief successful career as a model, Grace Kelly absolutely refused to pose for lingerie ads. Always protective of her ladylike image, she agreed to appear in an Old Gold cigarettes ad in a short skirt—until she saw the photographs. She vetoed them and insisted on retakes in a long skirt.

MAGGI NOLAN'S "CELEBRITY BULLETIN"

Princess Grace subscribed to the "Celebrity Bulletin" service sent out every day from Paris by Maggi Nolan to journalists and anyone else interested in knowing what celebrities were in

Paris. The bulletin enabled Grace to find out who had arrived in Paris and where they were staying.

Many were people she had known as an actress. She knew from experience most would be too shy to write her a note or telephone her at the palace. She was lonely. She missed Hollywood shop talk and American gossip. Rather than wait for the phone calls that would never come, she got in touch with them, inviting them to visit her in Monaco.

LINDA NORDLEY

The name of Grace Kelly's character in *Mogambo* was Linda Nordley, the sexually repressed Englishwoman who accompanied her anthropologist husband on safari in Africa and fell prey to the wildest game of all—white hunter Clark Gable. The role was in many ways thankless. Linda was insufferably condescending to Ava Gardner's good-time girl, Honey Bear. Her strident uppa-uppa-class accent was right on target as she trilled endlessly about how thrilling it was to be in Africa. When she fell for Gable, her metamorphosis into a woman crazed with passion was believable and touching. When, at the end, she found Gable and Gardner together, her pain and bewilderment synthesized her naïveté and made her shooting of Gable inevitable.

While Grace Kelly's natural beauty could not be ignored or denied, she stuck scrupulously to Linda Nordley's character by dressing in an ultraconservative style and wearing her hair in a tight bun covered with the kind of head scarf favored by the British royal family. Convincing in her panic, she managed to make moviegoers feel sorry for her yet glad that she and her husband were leaving and that Gable and Gardner would perhaps live happily ever after.

"NOT A FAIRY TALE"

Shortly before her death, Princess Grace told *People* magazine, "I certainly don't think of my life as a fairy tale. I think of

Princess Grace attending a formal function in the late 1970s.

myself as a modern contemporary woman who has had to deal
with all kinds of problems that many women today have to deal
with. I am still coping—trying to cope."

"NOT LOVE AT FIRST SIGHT," RAINIER ADMITS

In 1976, after twenty years of marriage, Prince Rainier confessed to top journalist Curtis Bill Pepper, "It was not love at first sight." Recalling his brief meeting with Grace at his palace in Monaco and the three-day whirlwind courtship in Philadelphia and New York that culminated in his proposal and their engagement, Rainier added, "Ours was a gradual falling in love. We were both ready for marriage."

NOT THE FIRST PRINCE OF MONACO TO MARRY AN AMERICAN

Prince Rainier's great grandfather, Prince Albert I (1848–1922), an oceanographer of world renown, was the first prince of Monaco to marry an American. She was Alice Heine. Born in New Orleans, she was his second wife and was not Rainier's great grandmother.

NOTABLES WHO ATTENDED GRACE'S FUNERAL

Among those attending the funeral services in Monaco for Princess Grace were Nancy Reagan, the Princess of Wales, President of Ireland Patrick Hillery, Prince Bertil of Sweden, Princess Benedikta of Denmark, Prince Bernhardt of the Netherlands, Grand Duchess Josephine of Luxembourg, film mogul Sam Spiegel, racing driver Jackie Stewart, Cary and Barbara Grant, and Barbara Sinatra.

NOTES FROM HER HIGH SCHOOL YEARBOOK

Grace Kelly graduated from the Stevens School in 1947. Her graduation yearbook listed her favorite orchestra as Benny Goodman's, favorite vocalist as Jo Stafford, favorite actor as Joseph Cotten, favorite actress as Ingrid Bergman, and favorite food as hamburgers.

AN OFFERING TO SAINTE-DEVOTE

Following the wedding ceremony uniting her with Prince Rainier, the new Princess Grace left the magnificent Cathedral of St. Nicholas and stopped for a moment at the modest little Church of Sainte-Dévote, Monaco's patron saint. As an offering, she left her spray of lilies of the valley on the altar.

THE OFFICIAL ANNOUNCEMENT OF THE ENGAGEMENT

On Thursday, January 5, 1956, the official announcement of the engagement of Grace Kelly to Prince Rainier III was made simultaneously in Monte Carlo and Philadelphia.

Announcing their engagement (left to right): Margaret Kelly, Prince Rainier III, Grace Kelly, Jack Kelly.

A rare publicity still of Grace Kelly from MGM.

AN OLD SKIRT AND A MAN'S SHIRT

When 20th Century–Fox asked Grace to test for a role in a film called *Taxi*, she walked into director Gregory Ratoff's office wearing the old skirt and man's shirt she habitually wore to class at the American Academy of Dramatic Arts. "She's perfect!" Ratoff screamed. "What I love about this girl is she's not pretty!"

The powers that were turned Grace down, but her test proved to be a breakthrough. Director John Ford saw it and hired her for *Mogambo*. Alfred Hitchcock saw it and was so impressed he cast her in *Dial M for Murder* and later in *Rear Window* and *To Catch a Thief*, explaining, "From the *Taxi* test, you could see Grace's potential for restraint. Grace has this control. It's a rare thing for a girl at such an age."

OLEG OGLES GRACE

Designer Oleg Cassini's first live sighting of Grace Kelly was in 1954 at Le Veau d'Or, a chic Manhattan bistro where she was dining with her current lover, the French heartthrob actor Jean-Pierre Aumont. Cassini had seen her on the screen and was determined to meet her. Later he described her as "a very aristocratic looking girl," gorgeous but not as striking as his ex-wife the actress Gene Tierney had been. He recalled in his memoirs, "the utter perfection of her nose . . . the long elegant neck . . . the silky diaphonous blonde hair," and that she wore "a black velvet two-piece, very demure, with a full skirt and a little white Peter Pan collar."

Although Cassini and Aumont knew each other, Aumont sensed Cassini was a marauder and tried to avoid introducing his companion. Cassini outmaneuvered him. It was all Cassini needed to begin his pursuit.

OLIVER AT SEA

Grace Kelly's black French poodle, Oliver, traveled with her to Monaco aboard the USS *Constitution* in April 1956 and settled happily into his new home in the Grimaldi palace with a free run of the luxuriant royal gardens.

OLIVER'S DEATH

Princess Grace's beloved black poodle, Oliver, died tragically in 1960 while the family was vacationing in Switzerland. Bouncy, inquisitive, and affectionate, he made the mistake of wandering away from the chalet into a deserted area, where he was attacked by a pack of wild dogs, leaving his mistress horror-struck

Arriving in New York in 1954 with Liz Taylor and Laraine Day, Grace, as usual, is carrying poodle Oliver. (UPI/Bettmann)

and inconsolable. The pet had been one of her few remaining links with her days as a single woman living in New York. He had traveled with her to Monaco in 1956 and was cradled in Grace's arms when she stepped on Monaco soil as the future consort of Prince Rainier.

Princess Grace wears her trademark turban and dark glasses during a visit to New York in the 1970s.

ON TURNING FORTY

With her fortieth birthday looming, a still flawlessly beautiful Princess Grace candidly expressed her emotional depression. In an interview with journalist William B. Arthur for *Look* magazine, she confessed, "I'm an absolute basket case. I can't stand it. It comes as a great jolt. It really does. It hits one right between the eyes. . . .

"For a woman, [forty] is torture, the end."

ONASSIS MAD WITH JOY

On hearing of Grace Kelly's engagement to Prince Rainier, Aristotle Onassis, whose investments in Monaco would be enriched by an heir to Monaco's throne, announced, "I am mad with joy!" Putting his money where his mouth was, he donated a million francs to the Monaco Red Cross. The practical reason for his joy was the fact that a probable heir guaranteed Monaco's tax-free status as per a treaty between Monaco and France.

THE 101-GUN SALUTE

On March 14, 1958, all of Monaco was awaiting the birth of Grace and Rainier's second child. Everyone hoped for a boy, not for any sexist reasons but because a treaty between Monaco and France said the principality would forfeit its independence and revert to France if Rainier did not produce a male heir. When the cannon went off at Fort Sainte Antoine, everyone counted to twenty-one, the gun salute traditionally honoring a female offspring. At the sound of the twenty-second shot, the entire principality exploded in thankfulness that built into hysteria as a 101-gun salute welcomed the royal son and heir, His Royal Highness Prince Albert Alexandre Louis Pierre, Duc de Valentois, Comte de Carlades, Baron du Buis, Seigneur de Saint Remy, Sire de Matignon, Comte de Torrigini, Baron de Saint Lo, Baron de Bambye, Baron de la Luthumière, Duc de Mazarin, Duc de Mayenne, Prince de Château Porcien, Baron d'Altkirch, Marquis de Chilly, Baron de Massy, and Marquis de Guiscard.

128 GIRLFRIENDS FOR ALBERT?

In 1991 the *Daily Express* newspaper of London reported that Prince Albert's roster of girlfriends added up to 128. Among his "acknowledged" friendships were Italian television hostess Gabiria Brandimarte and actresses Cathy Lee Crosby, Kim Alexis, Brooke Shields, and Catherine Alric, who allegedly ended their relationship with a note that read, "Love without faithfulness is like a flower without sun."

ONE OF THE SEVEN MOST FAMOUS WOMEN OF THE 1960s

According to celebrity biographer Maurice Zolotow, Princess Grace ranked among the seven most-written-about women in the early 1960s. The other six were Marilyn Monroe, Brigitte Bardot, Elizabeth Taylor, Jacqueline Kennedy, Princess Margaret, and Queen Elizabeth II.

ONE PRINCESS AND TWO LADIES ALL IN "WAITING"

In the autumn of 1956 Princess Grace and two of her best friends and bridesmaids were all pregnant. In due course, Princess Caroline, Rita Gam Guinzburg's Kate, and Judy Kanter's Amy were born.

THE ONLY MAN WHO WALKED OUT ON HER

Clark Gable was the only one of the many men in Grace Kelly's life who literally left her waiting at the gate. The love affair that began in Africa during the filming of *Mogambo* ended at the departure gate at London's Heathrow Airport. The date was April 15, 1953. Grace was on her way back to the States. Gable drove her to the airport where reporters were assembled for the Big farewell. When Gable kissed her good-bye, Grace knew it was a final good-bye and burst into tears. Three months later she had recovered sufficiently to start seeing French actor Jean-Pierre Aumont.

ONYX

Onyx was the name of Princess Caroline's black-and-brown shepherd dog, who proved to be an enormous comfort to her after her mother's death in 1982.

THE "ORIGINAL" GRACELAND

Throughout Princess Grace's reign, friends jokingly described Monte Carlo as the "original" Graceland as compared to Elvis Presley's Memphis domain.

"OUR" SONG

Every romance has a song the two lovers regard as "our" song. For Grace Kelly and Prince Rainier in the heady period of their engagement during Christmas week of 1955 and through the first months of 1956 before their wedding, "their" song was "Your Eyes Are the Eyes of a Woman in Love" from *Guys and Dolls*.

AN OUTPOURING OF SYMPATHY FROM AMERICA

In the weeks following Princess Grace's death, Prince Rainier and the family received twenty-four thousand letters of sym-

People *magazine's cover tribute to Princess Grace, September 27, 1982, edition.* (From *People*. People Weekly is a registered trademark of the Time Inc. Magazine Company, used with permission.)

pathy from Americans. Many wanted the Grimaldis to know they had arranged for special Masses to be said in local Catholic churches.

A PAINFUL MOMENT FOR AVA

Ava Gardner's father died of a lingering bronchial disease when she was fifteen, but she didn't feel the full impact of her loss until the day of her friend Grace Kelly's wedding. Recalling the painful moment in her autobiography, she wrote, "I found out how much I missed him, found out that some part of me lay in that grave with him. . . . At Grace Kelly's wedding in Monaco, I watched her strong, vibrant father walk her down the aisle, and I couldn't help but think, if only I had a father like him to lean on."

Clearly Ava had no idea how much Grace suffered from her father's cruel indifference and cutting sarcasm. A grim example of the grass always being greener. . . .

PALAIS PRINCIER

Palais Princier is how the prince's palace appears on local maps of Monaco.

THE PALATINE CHAPEL

After her death the body of Princess Grace lay in state in the Palatine Chapel of the royal palace, surrounded by banks of white flowers and three-foot-high candles. A guard of honor in plumed helmets and dress white uniforms stood stiffly at attention throughout a two-day vigil, wearing black armbands on their left arms in stark contrast to the white fabric.

"PAPPY"

Prince Rainier's grandchildren's pet name for him is "Pappy."

A PARAKEET NAMED HENRY

Until the Cary Grants gave her the poodle puppy named Oliver, Grace Kelly's only pet in her New York apartment in 1950 was a parakeet named Henry.

GISELE PASCAL AND GARY COOPER

Actor Gary Cooper's womanizing may have played a role in Prince Rainier's courtship of Grace Kelly in 1955. A year earlier, Prince Rainier had ended his long-term relationship with his French actress mistress Gisele Pascal because, among other things, she was having an affair with Gary Cooper.

Thus in one of life's strange ironies, Grace's first leading man and first "important" lover was indirectly instrumental in freeing the man she would marry from a personal entanglement.

PATERNITY SUIT THREAT

In 1991 German model Bea Fiedler announced to the press that she was filing a multimillion-dollar paternity suit against Prince Albert based on a one-night stand. Described in the European press as a "sex starlet," Fiedler subsequently announced that she would drop the suit if Albert would consent to let her "be with him." Prince Albert did not dignify the woman's allegations or the media coverage with a response of any kind. As quickly as the storm blew up, it faded away.

"PETITE COQUINE" (LITTLE SCAMP)

When Princess Caroline was a toddler, her mischievousness and charm inspired the palace staff to nickname her "petite coquine," which translates roughly as "little scamp."

PHILIPPE ON THE GALAPAGOS CRUISE

In the summer of 1977 Prince Rainier invited Philippe Junot to join the family on a cruise to the Galapagos Islands in the South Atlantic. Princess Caroline was in love with Junot and desperately wanted to marry him. Rainier wanted to get to know him better, and the cruise presented an ideal way to do it. Junot's charm, wit, and evident affection for Caroline in the close quarters of an ocean cruise convinced Rainier to allow the engagement to be announced on August 25 after they returned home.

PINOT DI PINOT

Stefano Casiraghi's powerboat *Pinot di Pinot* flipped over during a championship race in the waters of the Mediterranean off the coast of the French Riviera. Casiraghi was trapped and drowned before he could be rescued. The date was October 3, 1990, a mere six years after he and Princess Caroline were married. Widowed at thirty-three with three small children, a grief-stricken Caroline could not forget that Stefano had promised to give up powerboat racing—after the October 3 race!

PLACES GRACE LIVED

As a Child: By the time Grace was born, Jack Kelly had built (with Kelly bricks) the impressive fifteen-room house at 3901 Henry Avenue in the Germantown section of Philadelphia. This was where she grew up and where Prince Rainier asked her father for her hand in marriage. It continued to be the Kelly family home, where Grace and Rainier took their children on visits.

As an Actress: On arrival in New York in 1947, she moved into the Barbizon Hotel for Women at 140 East Sixty-Third Street, where "young ladies" of good families were considered to be in a safe and caring environment. As she began to earn money modeling, she moved into a small apartment in a new building erected with Kelly bricks called Manhattan House at 200 East Sixty-Sixth Street. With success came a glorious apartment at 988 Fifth Avenue near the Metropolitan Museum of Art, her last permanent New York residence before moving to Monaco.

In Hollywood, Grace shared an apartment on Sweetzer Avenue with close friend and future bridesmaid Rita Gam. At one point she rented a luxurious Hollywood house owned by MGM's talent head Lucille Ryman Carroll but rarely stayed there.

As Princess Grace: Her main residence was the pink royal palace built on the rock overlooking the Mediterranean Sea. The Grimaldis also had a "country" house, Roc Agel, in the French Alps adjacent to Monaco, from which Grace and Stephanie set out the day of Grace's fatal accident. For vacations the Grimaldis maintained a ski house in Gstaad, Switzerland, and often visited the Kelly family summer house on Wesley Avenue in Ocean City, New Jersey.

In Paris the Grimaldis maintained an apartment on fashionable avenue Foch. In London they stayed at the Connaught Hotel and in New York at the Regency Hotel.

PLASTIC SURGEON'S INSPIRATION

Santa Monica's "plastic surgeon to the stars," Dr. Steven M. Hoefflin, said in 1991, nearly a decade after her death, that the face that most inspires him is Grace Kelly's. Citing her large curvaceous eyes and attractive nose, he said, "Her cheekbones and smooth jawline were well-defined but natural, her features radiated strength and intelligence."

THE PLOT TO KIDNAP PRINCESS STEPHANIE

In November 1984 in Paris, Princess Stephanie, nineteen, was just pulling into the family garage when a man reached through the car window and put a gun to her head. She later recalled that her body turned to jelly but her mind continued to function. She was trying to push the man away when his female accomplice appeared at the other side of the car yelling, "Shoot her! Shoot her!" Trying to reason with them, Stephanie suggested they all go upstairs and talk to her father. "Nobody's going to pay for a dead body." The incident ended as quickly as it started. The would-be kidnappers lost their nerve and ran away. "I was a mess!"

PLOT TO SNATCH BODY FOILED

On October 3, 1991, the first anniversary of Stefano Casiraghi's death, two intruders broke through the seven-foot-high gate surrounding Monaco's Chapelle de la Paix, where he and other nonruling members of Monaco's royal family are entombed. As they attempted to break into the tomb itself, police rushed to the scene, but the intruders got away.

All was well except for one thing. The would-be body snatchers phoned the French news agency, Agence France Presse in Marseilles, saying they had in fact stolen Stefano's coffin. AFP editors notified a Monaco official, who was so overwrought he telephoned Princess Caroline in Paris before verifying the report.

The princess was inconsolable for hours until another phone call assured her the story was false; her late husband's mortal remains were safe.

THE POEM ON JACK KELLY'S WALL

One insight into Jack Kelly's character may be deduced from the framed poem he kept on the wall of his study. According to Kelly family friend John McCallum, the last of its five stanzas reads:

Dreamers have dared what the many feared
And conquered in spite of the men who jeered
For the joys that are and the things we know
Were the dreams of the few in the long ago.

The poem suggests Jack Kelly and his daughter Grace had more in common than they realized.

A POET AT FOURTEEN

Like many adolescent girls, Grace Kelly wrote poetry, some serious, some she described as "little gooney ones." One, written at age fourteen, is a sweet adolescent example:

Grace's love of poetry continued to grow throughout her life and offered her an outlet for her still-active creative yearnings. She often read at poetry recitals, including one at the Edinburgh Arts Festival in September 1976. (Stewart Ferguson/Camera Press London)

I hate to see the sun go down
And squeeze itself into the ground,
Since some warm night it might get stuck
And in the morning not get up.

THE POPE'S REPRESENTATIVE

His Excellency the Most Reverend Paul Marella, the Apostolic Nuncio of Paris, attended Grace and Rainier's civil and religious marriage ceremonies in his official capacity as the personal representative of Pope Pius XII.

PRAYING AT LOURDES

In 1979 the government of France chose Princess Grace and her son, Prince Albert, twenty-one, as its official representatives to the holy shrine at Lourdes, where they were photographed at prayer in the grotto.

PREGNANCIES

Princess Grace got pregnant on her honeymoon. Princess Caroline was born nine months and five days after the wedding. Prince Albert followed fourteen months later in 1958. Seven years of untold numbers of miscarriages followed until Princess Stephanie joined the family in 1965.

PRESIDENT OF THE MONACO RED CROSS

Prince Rainier had for several years been president of the Monaco Red Cross. Shortly after his marriage he turned the presidency over to Princess Grace. It soon became her top-priority responsibility. She expanded its programs to include day-care centers for working mothers, a center for orphans, infant care for expectant mothers, and first-aid training.

THE PRINCE AS ALTAR BOY

From early childhood, Prince Albert has been the most devoutly religious of Grace and Rainier's three children. As an adolescent in the early 1970s, he served as an altar boy in the palace chapel. He attended Mass regularly during his four years at Amherst College and later accompanied his mother to Lourdes in 1979.

PRINCE ELVIS?

While awaiting the birth of their first child, Grace and Rainier visited her family in Philadelphia. A local newspaper reporter asked them if they had chosen a name for the baby. Prince Rainier, in a joking mood, said, "We've only decided what not to name it. . . . I will never name the child Elvis!"

PRINCESS ALEXANDRA

Princess Alexandra was the name of the character played by Grace Kelly in The Swan, the 1956 film based on a Ferenc Molnár fable about a beautiful young fairy-tale princess torn between duty and love. The role of Princess Alexandra was totally at odds with the real-life role of the about-to-be Princess Grace. Molnár's Alexandra was born a princess and had led a sheltered, virginal life in her family's Ruritanian country house in the period before World War I. The plot revolved around her arranged betrothal to Crown Prince Albert, played by Alec Guinness, and her awakening passion for the music tutor played by Louis Jourdan.

At age twenty-six, Grace Kelly nevertheless conveyed the breathtaking innocence of an eighteen-year-old on the brink of discovering her womanhood. Her fragile beauty and exquisite wardrobe added a special romantic twist to the film's appeal when it opened at the end of April mere days after Grace Kelly became Her Serene Highness Princess Grace of Monaco.

PRINCESS GRACE IN BRONZE

A magnificent bronze statue of Princess Grace lends her eternal presence to the Princess Grace Rose Garden in the Fontvieille section of Monaco. Inaugurated on June 18, 1984, nearly two years after her death, the garden was dedicated to her memory in a simple ceremony led by Prince Rainier and her children. A quiet spot fragrant with the scent of some thirty-five hundred rose bushes and more than 150 varieties of roses, the garden is open to the public from sunrise to sunset. Many visitors arrive just before sunrise to enjoy the special moment of nature's beauty when the sun comes up.

"PRINCESS GRACE REMEMBERED"

Shortly before her death in 1982, Princess Grace was asked by her friend Mstislav Rostropovich to participate in a fund-raising concert in Washington, D.C., in March 1983. Her role was to have been the narration for The Carnival of Animals, a National Symphony Orchestra concert at the John F. Kennedy Center for the Performing Arts; its goal was to raise money for the orchestra's pension fund.

Because of her death, the concert was performed in memory of Princess Grace and was shown on television six months later on September 26, 1983, as part of PBS's "Great Performances" series. Its title was "Princess Grace Remembered." As substitute narrator, First Lady Nancy Reagan, herself a former actress, was critically well received.

A PRINCESS GRACE TRIBUTE TO CARY GRANT

On October 19, 1988, an all-star roster of celebrities gathered at the Beverly Hilton Hotel in Los Angeles for the Princess Grace Foundation Special Gala Tribute to Cary Grant. Among those in attendance were friends and family of both Grace and Cary: Michael Caine, Eva Marie Saint, Gregory Peck, Liza Minnelli, Judith Balaban Quine, Dina Merrill, Roger Moore, Frank Sinatra, Merv Griffin, Robert J. Wagner, Shirley Temple Black, Quincy Jones, Henry Mancini—and Prince Rainier, Prince Albert, and Princess Stephanie of Monaco along with Cary Grant's beautiful young widow, Barbara.

PRINCESS MARILYN OF MONACO

In 1955, before Prince Rainier met Grace Kelly, Monaco was going through an economic slump. Aristotle Onassis suggested the prince marry an American film star. Ari's friend, magazine publisher Gardner Cowles, half-seriously suggested Marilyn Monroe. When approached, Marilyn said she liked the idea but didn't know where Monaco was. She was considering meeting Rainier when he announced his engagement.

PRINCIPALITY OF MONACO: A BRIEF EIGHT-HUNDRED-YEAR HISTORY

From earliest antiquity, the Rock of Monaco and its natural harbor served as a refuge for local tribes and for the first traders in the Mediterranean. In the sixth century B.C. it was inhabited by a Ligurian tribe that the Greeks called the Monoikos (the probable origin of the name Monaco). In 122 B.C. the Romans settled in Provence, and Monaco became part of the Alpes-Maritimes. Julius Caesar sailed from Monaco in his campaign against the Greeks. After the fall of the Roman Empire in A.D. 500, the region was ravaged by barbarians until the year 972, when the count of Provence crushed the Saracens, heralding the start of a new era.

In 1162 the Emperor Barbarossa gave maritime dominion over the region to the Republic of Genoa. For the next two hundred years Monaco was the scene of fierce fighting between two groups: the Ghibellines, who supported the emperor of Genoa, and the Guelfs, who were loyal to the pope.

Enter the Grimaldis: On January 8, 1297, François Grimaldi, loyal to the pope, secretly entered Monaco disguised as a monk, an event commemorated in the Grimaldi coat of arms by two monks brandishing swords. By the middle of the fourteenth century his descendant Charles Grimaldi was ruling Monaco and several nearby fiefdoms.

For the next four hundred years the Grimaldis managed to hang on to their power while Monaco itself survived the political "protection" of various European powers, including France and Spain.

Grimaldis Imprisoned: The low point in the family fortunes came in 1793, when French revolutionaries arrested the Grimaldi family, took its riches, turned the palace into a workhouse, and changed the name of Monaco to Fort Hercule. Nearly twenty years passed before the Treaty of Paris was signed in 1814, restoring the Grimaldis to power.

Modern Times: In 1865 the gambling casino was built; the next year the town of Monte Carlo was named. Over the next fifty years Monaco's citizens enjoyed the privileges of not paying taxes of any kind. By 1911, the principality had a democratic constitution and was known for its scientific institutions founded by Prince Albert I, Prince Rainier III's great grandfather, and for such cultural activities as the first performances of Sergey Diaghilev's Ballets Russes.

Prince Rainier III: Born in 1923, the son of Princess Charlotte and Count Pierre de Polignac, Prince Rainier III was educated in Britain and acceded to the throne in 1949, succeeding his grandfather, Prince Louis II. He and Grace Kelly met at his palace in 1955 during the nearby Cannes Film Festival and were married the following April. In the ensuing decades Monaco changed from a gambling resort to a thriving tourist, cultural, and international commerce center with luxurious housing, hotels, and convention accommodations. Princess Grace's interests ranged from the Red Cross, the La Leche League, gardens, and sports to ballet, theater, and music with year-round events supporting all of these areas.

Years of Grace: Grace Patricia Kelly was literally a dream come true for Monaco. According to a treaty with France, if Prince Rainier did not marry and produce an heir, the principality would revert to France at his death. In addition to this cloud was the economic reality of Monaco in the post–World War II years. Verging on bankruptcy, it needed a new image to attract tourists and investments. Her Serene Highness solved both problems by giving birth to three children—including the desired heir, Prince Albert—and by attracting business and cultural leaders to one of the smallest countries in the world.

Her death in September 1982 shattered the citizens of Monaco as well as her family, friends, and admirers worldwide.

PROUD NEW MOTHER

Eight months after Caroline's birth in 1957, Princess Grace said in an interview, "I must agree with people who say she's gorgeous. She weighs nineteen pounds now, has big fat cheeks and very long legs. She has dark blue eyes like her father and she's even getting more hair—with the beginning of a blond

Proud parents Grace and Rainier show off little Caroline to the crowds gathered below. (Edward Quinn/Globe Photos)

curl which we are coaxing along. She's got her first tooth, a bottom one, and she was pretty fussy when it came too. Now she's chewing everything she can get into her mouth . . . her bedclothes, all my beads, my husband's ties, and even the ears on our poodles."

QUALITY OVER QUANTITY

When Grace Kelly was preparing for her role as the coffee planation owner in *Green Fire*, Hungarian-born director Andrew Marton was reviewing her wardrobe. An assistant asked, "Shall we build up her front?" This was during the early 1950s emphasis on big breasts, which Grace clearly did not have. Marton was quick to reply, "No! I prefer quality to quantity!"

'RACE KELLY?

Alfred Hitchcock and Grace Kelly shared a passion for word games. After meeting the actress Lizabeth Scott, the director was amused by the notion of what would happen if other famous people dropped the first letter of their names: 'Rank Sinatra? 'Reer Garson? 'Ickey Rooney? It was a game that tickled the intellectual fancy of 'Race Kelly!

RAINIER AND GRACE CONVERSED IN ENGLISH

Although French was Rainier's first language, his English schooling gave him total fluency in English. Grace learned to speak French for official occasions but could always relax with her husband and converse in her native tongue.

RAINIER BUYS A PONY

Prince Rainier's purchase of a pony during Grace's first pregnancy in 1956 gave rise to speculation that his heart was set on a boy. Confronted with this suggestion, a furious father-to-be said it meant nothing of the kind and that girls as well as boys enjoyed riding a pony.

RAINIER DENIES MARRIAGE RUMORS

When the photographs of Grace and Rainier taken at their first meeting in Monaco appeared in *Paris Match* in September 1955, rumors of an impending marriage were so intense that the prince took to the airwaves. Word had spread that the meeting was not their first, that a courtship had been conducted in secret, and that perhaps they were already married.

On October 11, 1955, Rainier went on Radio Monte Carlo to assure his citizens that any rumors they might have heard were only that, rumors, and that the press reports were simply not true.

What was true, however, was his arrangement with Grace to meet in America at Christmastime.

RAINIER HAS A FIT WHEN GRACE CUTS HER HAIR

Prince Rainier did not approve of the way Princess Grace looked with short hair. When she had it cut in 1957, thinking it would be easier to manage, Rainier—like many husbands—had a fit. Grace had no choice but to let it grow. She dealt with the continuing problem of fine, difficult-to-manage tresses with the collection of hairpieces created for her by hairstylist M. Alexandre of Paris.

RAINIER HELPED WITH THE DISHES

When Prince Rainier visited Philadelphia in December 1955 in order to meet Grace Kelly's family, her sister Lizanne and her husband, Don, invited the courting couple to their little apartment for dinner. As Lizanne recalled thirty-two years later in the TV film documentary "Grace Kelly: The American Princess," "He fit in very well . . . even helped with the dishes."

RAINIER IGNORES THE MATCHMAKERS

Three years after Princess Grace's death, Prince Rainier was said to be courting one of Europe's most sophisticated beauties, the twice-divorced Princess Ira von Furstenberg. The press waited. The prince declined to comment. Nothing happened.

RAINIER SHOCKED

In the aftermath of his wife's death, Prince Rainier was shocked by the persistent suggestions that Princess Stephanie had been driving the car in which she and her mother were returning to Monaco from their farm. He was also distressed that the tragedy would diminish Monaco's attraction for tourists. In an exclusive interview with *Life* magazine's managing editor, Richard B. Stolley, His Serene Highness said Princess Grace "was of course a great attraction for tourists, she had great appeal. She did a lot for the glamour and prestige of the princi-

Grace's children continue the work their mother began, representing the royal family at cultural and state functions. (Rex Features London)

pality, but I don't think her disappearance means that people are not going to come.

"They didn't come only for that. They came for the whole atmosphere which we will try to carry on."

As a father, he admitted that he thought the speculation was not nice for Grace's children, who were doing their best to take on her special responsibilities, primarily the cultural events—ballet, theater, and opera—and the Monaco Red Cross.

RAINIER'S "IDEAL WOMAN"

In December 1955, shortly before leaving Monaco for a visit to the United States, the bachelor Prince Rainier described his ideal woman as "a girl who is fair-haired with the sort of subtle beauty that grows on you. She has long, flowing hair and her eyes are blue or hazel flecked with gold."

She had to be unspoiled, he told *Collier's* magazine interviewer David Schoenbrun, not a glossy beauty, "an intelligent
girl but not an intellectual. There's nothing more disagreeable
to a man than having a wife who knows more than he does on
every subject. It's even worse than being beaten at tennis. . . ."

RAINIER'S MOTHER MARRIES AN EX-CON

Late in her life, Rainier's mother, Princess Charlotte, devoted
her considerable energies to the rehabilitation of ex-convicts. A
short time before her death she married one of them, whom she
had originally hired as a chauffeur at her Château de Marchais
in northern France.

RAINIER'S PALACE IN THE BACKGROUND

One of Grace Kelly's love scenes with Cary Grant in *To Catch a
Thief* shows her future home, Prince Rainier's palace, in the
background. She did not meet her future husband until a year
after the 1954 filming, when she returned to the Riviera to
attend the 1955 Cannes Film Festival.

RAINIER'S PARENTS WERE DIVORCED

His mother, Princess Charlotte, divorced his father, French
count Pierre de Polignac, in 1933. Although she was heir to her
father Prince Louis's throne, she renounced her rights in favor
of her son, Rainier. When Prince Louis died in 1949, his
twenty-four titles, considerable bank account, and one-man rule
of Monaco skipped a generation and went to his grandson,
Rainier.

RAVENHILL CONVENT SCHOOL

Between the ages of six and fourteen, Grace Kelly attended the
straitlaced Ravenhill Convent School located near the Kellys'
Germantown home. Two of the teaching nuns reminisced about
her in later years. According to Sister Elizabeth Mary Blint,

Grace displayed her flair for acting at age six when she portrayed the Blessed Mother in the school's annual nativity play. Dressed in a long, flowing white gown, she amazed everyone with her poise, dignity, and the way she projected her strong little voice. "She cradled and caressed Baby Jesus, making you believe it was a real baby instead of a doll. At the end of the performance, she curtsied to a standing ovation."

In contrast was Grace's more "devilish" side as recalled by Sister Marie Dorothy, who taught Grace a few years later at the age of twelve. "I can still picture her sitting at the back of the class, laughing, giggling and telling her classmates dirty jokes while I was trying to teach."

THE RED CROSS COSTUME BALL

Princess Grace established the annual Red Cross Ball in Monaco as one of the most glamorous—and lucrative—fund-raising events of the year. The international set loved putting on lavish costumes and giving lavish sums of money to a good cause. Among her Hollywood chums who regularly attended were Frank Sinatra, Sophia Loren, Gina Lollobrigida, and Richard Burton. Grace herself loved dressing up. One year her headpiece had golden spikes and extended several feet on either side. She could not fit into a car. Instead she had to be driven to the gala in a truck.

RELAXING WITH RAINIER

Away from the demands of state, Prince Rainier enjoys driving a tractor and tinkering with wrought iron in his workshop at the family farm. Like his American in-laws, he likes to barbecue steaks outdoors for his family and friends.

Princess Grace as an eighteenth-century French aristocrat at a 1970s costume ball, clearly a role she had no trouble playing.

RELUCTANTLY TURNS DOWN THE POPE

Early in 1982 Princess Grace was approached to costar in a London stage production of a play written by Pope John Paul II as a young man. According to *People* magazine, she was the pontiff's personal choice. Grace begged off. "To act, to have a career and to do it well you have to do it completely. I don't have the time to devote to it."

RENDEZVOUS ON SKIS

In March 1992 Princess Caroline and French actor Vincent Lindon tried to have a secret rendezvous at the Swiss ski resort Zürs. Caroline and her three children—Andrea, seven, Charlotte, five, and Pierre, four—stayed at the elegant Lorunser Hotel. Leaving the children with instructors at the kiddie slope, Caroline then took the chair lift to the top of the mountain, where Lindon had arrived separately. Unhappily for their planned privacy, the paparazzi caught up with them, and photographs of them in their winter wonderland appeared around the world.

REPRESENTING PRINCE RAINIER ABROAD

In 1991 Prince Rainier sent his thirty-three-year-old son and heir, Prince Albert, to Japan as his official representative at the enthronement of Emperor Akihito. Pleased with reports of his son's performance, Rainier sent him abroad again the following year to attend the funeral of Norway's King Olav.

A RHINOCEROS NAMED MARGARET

Prince Rainier's love of animals is well established. At one point the family farm Roc Agel boasted four llamas, a hippopotamus named Pollux, and a rhinoceros he bought in England named Margaret. Today the animals live at the Monaco Zoo.

Prince Rainier shows his pet chimpanzee to his sister, Princess Antoinette, in 1955.

ROC AGEL

In 1956, following his marriage, Prince Rainier bought a mountaintop farm behind Monaco named Roc Agel. He personally worked the land, planting four hundred trees, clearing the paths around the property, and driving a bulldozer himself. At twenty-three hundred feet above sea level, it is often veiled in clouds. What most appealed to Princess Grace was its privacy. There was no way a photographer could peer down on the farm from above except from a helicopter, which could be heard and shooed away. She once described Roc Agel as the place "where we close the door to the world."

It was from a pleasant weekend at Roc Agel that Princess Grace and Princess Stephanie departed on the journey that ended in Grace's death.

THE ROCK (LE ROCHER)

The Rock is the high promontory overlooking Monte Carlo harbor where the Grimaldi royal palace now stands. From ancient times, because of its position, there has always been a fortification of some kind on this spot. Over the centuries it has been occupied by Phoenicians, Ligurians, Romans, Saracens, Genoese, and finally, the Grimaldis.

A ROCKING HORSE FROM DE GAULLE

On a visit to Monaco in the early sixties, French president and Mrs. Charles de Gaulle arrived at the palace with gifts for the children, including a red rocking horse for Prince Albert. Knowing that her son already had a red rocking horse exactly like the new one, Grace was nervous that either little Albert would say he already had one or the de Gaulles would decide to visit the nursery and see that their generous gift was not original. Thinking fast, she whispered to her lady-in-waiting to hurry to the nursery to conceal the rocking horse. There was no way to signal a child as young as Albert. But miraculously he accepted the de Gaulles' gift with childish enthusiasm and never mentioned its twin in the nursery.

Like most older people who bring gifts for children, the de Gaulles were thrilled when the children liked them.

THE ROYAL FOOTMEN

Of the more than one hundred men and women in service at the royal palace in Monaco, ten are classified as footmen in personal attendance on the family. Dressed handsomely as if chorus members of a lavish nineteenth-century opera, they wear green-striped jackets and trousers with red waistcoats embellished with gold buttons for their everyday responsibilities. On state occasions, however, they wear full livery with velvet knee breeches, white silk stockings, and buckled shoes.

ROYAL HOME DELIVERY

Princess Grace chose to have each of her three children at home at the palace rather than in a hospital. As a supporter of the La Leche League, she breast-fed all of them.

THE ROYAL PAIN-IN-THE-JEANS PROBLEM

American blue jeans were considered chic attire by Princess Stephanie and her Eurotrash friends—but not by Princess Grace. On one occasion at the palace Stephanie showed up for luncheon in jeans instead of the dress she was expected to wear. Grace insisted she change. Stephanie's response was to stay in jeans and miss the luncheon.

Another time in London, Caroline and some chums showed up at the elegant Connaught Hotel in Mayfair, where Grace was in residence. The young people, wearing blue jeans and sweaters, attempted to order breakfast in the restaurant but were turned away for not being properly attired. An outraged Caroline got on the house phone with her mother. "Just because we've got on jeans they won't give us breakfast." Grace answered, "Perfectly right, dear," and hung up.

"ROYALTY DOESN'T MEAN A THING TO US"

When Prince Rainier asked Jack Kelly's permission to marry his daughter Grace, Kelly rather ungraciously remarked, "Royalty doesn't mean a thing to us." Rainier evidently took the remark in good humor, although his future father-in-law later recalled, "I told him that I certainly hoped he wouldn't run around the way some princes do, and I told him that if he did, he'd lose a mighty fine girl."

STAN RUBIN AND THE TIGERTOWN FIVE

The only American music group invited to perform in Monaco during the Grace-Rainier wedding festivities, Stan Rubin's

Dixieland jazz band consisted of Princeton University undergraduates and was the rage at debutante parties circa 1956.

RUMOR VEHEMENTLY DENIED!

At the time of Grace's engagement to Rainier, the gossip columns were rife with "insider" stories that the actress had
undergone a battery of humiliating gynecological examinations
to assure her fertility before she could become the prince's
consort. In later years her close women friends scoffed at the
suggestion, pointing out that there was no such thing as a quick
fertility test at that time. Since she became pregnant on her
honeymoon within days of her wedding, the subject was quickly
forgotten.

In his 1989 biography *Rainier and Grace*, close family friend
Jeffrey Robinson describes a personal discussion with Prince
Rainier on the subject. He quotes Rainier as insisting Grace
"didn't go through any medical tests whatsoever. As far as I
know, she didn't have a simple check-up before we got married.
And there definitely was no fertility test. Had she not been able
to bear children there was another option open to us. . . .
According to the treaty with France, should there be no natural
heir to the throne, the ruling sovereign may adopt a child to
perpetuate the reign."

A SAD CHRISTMAS CARD

Because of the death of Princess Caroline's husband, Stefano
Casiraghi, the official Grimaldi family Christmas card for 1990
replaced the traditional family portrait with a somber photograph of a lonely-looking Christmas tree in the palace courtyard.

A (partial) family portrait. Princess Grace, Prince Rainier, Prince Albert, and Princess Stephanie at the palace in Monaco about a year before her fatal accident.

"SADNESS AND DISAPPOINTMENT"

In 1975 Princess Grace told *People* weekly journalist Fred Hauptfuhrer, "I don't dwell on the past. I look forward. . . . I take my job seriously, but not myself. People who cannot be objective about themselves become confused. Every life has sadness and disappointments, but if one has any sense one thinks only of the good and forgets the bad. I have been very fortunate and very lucky."

SAINT-MAUR SCHOOL

Saint-Maur is the day school in Monte Carlo attended by Princess Caroline as a child and more recently by her three children, Andrea, Charlotte, and Pierre.

SAINTE-DEVOTE

Sainte-Dévote is Monaco's patron saint. According to legend, in the fourth century a frail skiff carrying the saint foundered on the rocky shore of what is now the Condamine section of the principality, leaving the saint to live out the remaining years of his life there. It wasn't until seven hundred years later that a votive chapel was built in honor of Sainte-Dévote, and another eight hundred years were to elapse before Prince Rainier's great great grandfather, Prince Charles III, restored and enlarged the ancient religious site in 1870.

January 26 is the designated saint's day. Each year on that date at dusk, a symbolic skiff is burned in front of the chapel as part of the ceremonies of a traditional ancient cult that still has its fervent worshipers.

JEANNIE SAKOL

Jeannie Sakol, coauthor of this book, attended the Grace Kelly–Prince Rainier wedding in April 1956 as a special correspondent for the National Broadcasting Company. Her assignment was to arrange for exclusive interviews for actress Arlene Francis, who was the host of the NBC-Home Show as well as a panelist on the CBS show "What's My Line." Among the interviews she arranged was one with literary giant W. Somerset Maugham at his Villa Mauresque at St.-Jean-Cap-Ferrat. Among her cherished belongings is Maugham's gift to her, a red leather-bound edition of his short-story collection *Cosmopolitans* inscribed "For Jeanne from the author of these little stories. W. Somerset Maugham."

While many who attended the wedding later scoffed at it as a badly staged circus, Jeannie found the entire experience romantic and exciting. She was among the cheering thousands at the harbor when Grace Kelly arrived clutching her black poodle Oliver as Prince Rainier guided her ashore. She sat in the clammy Cathedral of St. Nicholas during the religious ceremony, where she could see everything—but not hear a word.

Since that halcyon time, Sakol has authored several works of fiction and nonfiction, including four with Caroline Latham. Coproducer of the award-winning two-hour documentary *The Compleat Beatles*, she has also written for leading women's magazines.

Legendary British author W. Somerset Maugham welcomes NBC's Arlene Francis and Jeannie Sakol to his fabled Villa Mauresque at Cap Ferrat the day before he attended the wedding of Prince Rainier and Grace Kelly.

SARDINES BY CANDLELIGHT

David Niven and his wife Hjordis fulfilled their hearts' desire in the early 1960s by buying an old villa in the south of France. It was "an old monstrosity" according to David, perched in an olive grove on a little promontory of its own on Cap Ferrat.

Their nearby neighbors and old friends were Princess Grace and Prince Rainier of Monaco.

With furniture arriving piecemeal and the electricity yet to be connected, the Niven house was officially declared open one night by Her Serene Highness, who, as Niven later recalled, "sat on a packing case with her enchanting husband and ate sardines by candlelight."

A SEVERE CHILDHOOD STUTTER

Prince Albert had a severe childhood stutter that threatened to curtail his official public appearances as he reached his teenage years. A course in speech therapy gradually helped him overcome the problem. As an adult he has made countless speeches with nary a hint of a stutter.

THE SHAH OF IRAN'S GIFT

In 1949, when the shah of Iran visited New York for a week, a friend of the Kelly family, Manie Sachs, arranged for Grace to be his escort for a round of theaters, restaurants, and clubs. To show his appreciation, the shah gave her some magnificent jewelry from Van Cleef & Arpels as well as an enormous portrait of himself in a silver frame. The jewelry consisted of a gold bracelet watch with a dome of pearls and diamonds covering the watch face, a pin in the form of a gold birdcage containing a bird with a diamond body, and a solid gold vanity case eight inches long with thirty-two diamonds in the clasp. Although her mother demanded she return the jewelry, Grace refused. The portrait was displayed in her room at the Barbizon Hotel for Women for all to see and envy.

SHARE AND SHARE UNLIKE

Grace and Rainier had few interests in common.

She loved opera, ballet, and theater—indoor cultural activities.

He loved sailing, skin diving, old automobiles, and collecting wild animals.

She got seasick aboard her husband's boats.
He fell asleep during concerts.

"SHE CLUTCHES HER JEWEL BOX AND FLEES . . ."

Following *The Country Girl*, MGM offered Grace Kelly the heroine's role in a swashbuckling costume drama, *Quentin Durward*. After reading the script, she turned it down. "All I had to do was wear 35 different costumes and look frightened. The men were duelling and fighting but the stage directions for me said, 'She clutches her jewel box and flees. . . .' "

SHIP DRILL CANCELED BECAUSE OF GRACE

It wasn't her fault. Other passengers aboard the USS *Constitution* en route to the wedding in Monaco wanted a closer look at Grace Kelly. When the lifeboat drill was called, more than 250 of them tried to share her lifeboat station, which was designed for only 150.

Since nobody would budge, the drill was called off.

FRANK SINATRA

Grace Kelly's relationship with Frank Sinatra grew out of her friendship with Ava Gardner when the two actresses costarred with Clark Gable in *Mogambo* in 1953. Frank and Ava's marriage was at its rockiest at the time, because Ava's career was flourishing while Frank's had hit the skids. When he visited the *Mogambo* location in Africa, Frank was a stressed-out bundle of nerves, waiting to hear whether he was being given the role of Maggio in *From Here to Eternity*. He got the part, won an Academy Award, and catapulted once more into superstardom in films, concerts, and recordings. Sinatra's renewed success didn't save his marriage to Ava, although they both maintained their friendship with Grace. By the time of the royal wedding, they had officially separated (they would divorce in 1957). Both were invited to the wedding and its attendant festivities. Ava duly arrived to show her affection and support for the friend

Grace and Frank Sinatra prepare for a scene in High Society *in January 1956.* (UPI/Bettmann)

who was about to undertake the biggest "role" of her life. On the day of the wedding the Cathedral of St. Nicholas was packed with family, friends, and officials—except for one empty seat next to Ava Gardner.

As Frank later explained, he had gone to London, fitted himself out with the "correct" attire for the wedding, and was about to take off for Monaco when he abruptly changed his mind. The reason? The paparazzi and the gossip columnists were demanding to know if his joining Ava at Grace's wedding meant a reconciliation. He feared his arrival in Monte Carlo might disrupt the solemnity of the occasion as photographers stampeded to shoot Ava and him together.

Princess Grace forgave him, of course. After all, he had been her costar in her last film, *High Society*, and had become friends with Prince Rainier when he visited the set. During the next quarter of a century, until Grace's death, Sinatra was a frequent guest at the palace. Such was Grace's friendship with both Frank and Ava that when Princess Caroline married Philippe Junot, Frank and his new wife Barbara were among the guests, as was Ava Gardner. At a prewedding luncheon hosted by David Niven, Sinatra sang "My Way" to Caroline and Philippe.

The last time Frank and Grace saw each other was on March 31, 1982, in Philadelphia, when he and Barbara attended the "Tribute to Grace Kelly" at the Annenberg Center. The occasion was Philadelphia's tricentennial. The event was sponsored by the Century IV Commission. Stewart Granger and James Stewart were also on hand to honor their former leading lady. In a brief speech, Grace said, "I am overwhelmed and so filled with love, I would just like to hug every one of you."

Brief Bio: Francis Albert Sinatra was born in Hoboken, New Jersey, on December 12, 1917. His first radio appearance was in 1937 on the "Major Bowes Amateur Hour." As a band singer with Harry James and Tommy Dorsey, he caused the "bobby-soxers" of the early 1940s to "swoon" during personal appearance renditions of such romantic ballads as "This Love of Mine" and "I'll Never Smile Again." Sinatra's more than fifty years in the public eye have been a soap opera cavalcade of front-page professional and personal drama, including innumerable recordings that have become standards, more than sixty films, four marriages, and friendships with people ranging from underworld figures to Presidents Kennedy and Reagan.

Sinatra's 1939 marriage to Nancy Barbato produced three children: Tina, Nancy ("with the laughing eyes!"), and Frank, Jr. It ended in 1951 so he could marry Ava Gardner. That marriage also ended in divorce, in 1957. For the next nine years Frank romanced Juliet Prowse, Marilyn Monroe, and Lauren Bacall, who, after the death of husband Humphrey Bogart, expected to marry Frank and was unceremoniously dumped. Bacall later complained, "He behaved like a complete shit!" In

1966 he married actress Mia Farrow, twenty-eight years his junior. They divorced two years later. In 1977, after a four-year courtship, he married Zeppo Marx's glamorous blond widow, Barbara, and seemed to have found marital happiness at long last.

SIX MEN IN EIGHTEEN MONTHS

Between mid-1953 and the end of 1954, Grace Kelly costarred with six of Hollywood's biggest box office male stars: Clark Gable, Ray Milland, James Stewart, William Holden, Bing Crosby, and Cary Grant. As *Time* magazine commented at the beginning of 1955, "She is a star who was never a starlet, who never worked up from B pictures, never posed for cheesecake, was never elected with a press agent's help, Miss Antiaircraft Battery C. She was not discovered behind a soda fountain or at a drive-in."

Among the reasons the popular weekly gave for Grace's success at snagging the six most popular leading men was "She inspires licit passion."

SIXTY TV SHOWS IN TWO YEARS

In the early 1950s television dramas were presented live. Most productions originated in New York. While auditioning for Broadway, Grace Kelly managed to appear on more than sixty television shows in two years. Among the most famous ones were "Studio One," "Robert Montgomery Presents," "Kraft Playhouse," "Lux Video Theatre," "Hallmark Hall of Fame," and "Playhouse 90." In subsequent years this period of East Coast creativity before the advent of tape and canned audience reaction became known as the "Golden Age of Television."

SLAM BOOK

In 1943, a teenage fad was the slam book. It was a notebook in which young people wrote down their favorite loves and pet hates. The thirteen-year-old Grace Kelly had a slam book that she entrusted to her friend Jack Oeschle for safekeeping. Twelve years later in 1955, he revealed the contents in *Motion Picture* magazine. Grace had written that her favorite sport was swimming; her favorite actress, Ingrid Bergman; her favorite actor, Alan Ladd; her favorite comedian, Bob Hope; her pet hate, school.

"A SLOW AND CAREFUL DRIVER"

Responding to criticism of Princess Grace's driving several months after her fatal crash in September 1982, Prince Rainier said she was always "a slow and careful driver." He recalled that she was so slow and careful that when she offered her children a lift from the farm at Roc Agel back to the palace, they would tease her by saying they could get there quicker on foot!

"SMILE OF BEAUTY"

In 1949 Grace Kelly posed with a toothbrush in a bathroom setting for an Ipana toothpaste ad. The theme was the "smile of beauty." Her reason for posing was to pay for her acting lessons in New York.

GEORGE STACEY AND THE "KISSING CHAIR"

The interior designer Grace Kelly chose to decorate the Fifth Avenue apartment she moved into after filming *The Country Girl* in 1955 was George Stacey. As described by close friend and author Judith Balaban Quine, "The soft, fluid and feminine lines of newly acquired French antiques looked a great deal more like [Grace] than the neutered brown flat she had left, as did the colors—primarily a rich but pale blue—that dotted her ivory living room. The first piece of living room furniture you saw as you came through the front door was a gilded S-shaped settee where two people could face each other for conversation. It was covered in fabric that had the word 'love' woven into it, and we all called it the kissing chair."

GEORGE STACEY TO THE RESCUE

With her first baby due in a matter of weeks, Princess Grace was in despair because the palace nursery was not ready for occupancy. The renovation and decoration were in total disarray. That's when international interior designer George Stacey came to the rescue. They had met in New York when he decorated her Fifth Avenue apartment and had become friends.

Rushing to Monaco, he pulled things quickly into shape, using Grace's favorite color, yellow, because it was cheerful and would accommodate either a boy or a girl.

A STAINED SCULLING CAP FOR KING GEORGE

As a young man Jack Kelly became proficient enough at rowing to compete in the Diamond Sculls at Britain's Royal Henley Regatta in 1920. Just before leaving for Britain, he received official word that he was disqualified because he was not a "gentleman." Two months later at the Olympics, he defeated the Diamond Sculls winner and brought home a gold medal. To express his triumph and outrage (as well as wounded personal dignity), he sent his sweat-stained green sculling cap to Britain's King George V.

A STARK OPINION: "NO SEX APPEAL!"

After Oleg Cassini arranged a meeting in 1953 between Grace and powerful Hollywood agent Ray Stark with a view to his taking her on as a client, Stark told Cassini, "Sorry, Oleg. No sex appeal."

STEFANO

In 1983 Princess Caroline married Stefano Casiraghi, a tall, fair-haired, quiet Milanese three years her junior. The son of a wealthy industrialist, Stefano had an interest in an Italian shoe manufacturing company, making him the "perfect husband" according to Caroline since shoes were her passion. To please her, he had special labels made for her shoes that said they had been created exclusively for her.

Moving to Monaco after their marriage, he expanded his business interests to include real estate and boat building. He and Caroline talked of wanting six children. Three were born in quick succession: Andrea in 1984, Charlotte in 1986, Pierre in 1987. The family divided its time among Monaco, Paris, and Milan.

In 1989 Stefano won the World Championship Powerboat Race in Atlantic City, New Jersey. Because of the danger inherent in the sport, he had promised his wife that he would enter one more competition and then quit racing. On October 3, 1990, he and his friend Patrice Innocenti were copiloting their catamaran, *Pinot di Pinot*, defending Stefano's title of the previous year in a race off the Riviera coast. They were making a run at nearly a hundred miles per hour when the forty-two-foot boat struck a wave and overturned. Innocenti was thrown clear, but Stefano was trapped inside the boat underwater.

In a terrible twist of fate, two days before the accident Stefano had been disqualified from the race for stopping to help a competitor in trouble. But because he was one of the organizers of the event and a defending champion, the rules were waived.

STEFANO'S LAST BIRTHDAY PARTY

Mere weeks before his death Casiraghi and Princess Caroline took a planeload of fifty friends to Marrakech to celebrate his thirtieth birthday.

STEPHANIE AND MARIO

In 1987 Princess Stephanie became romantically involved with Mario Oliver Jutard, a twice-married former waiter from Marseilles who had a criminal record for sexually assaulting a nineteen-year-old student. She met him in Los Angeles. Despite Prince Rainier's disapproval, the affair lasted for two years. Jutard had proposed marriage, and she was considering it when she caught him making love to another, even younger woman.

STEPHANIE BANNED FROM CAROLINE'S WEDDING BALL

Princess Stephanie was a rebellious thirteen-year-old when big sister Caroline and Philippe Junot married in 1978. When she announced she would wear pants rather than a dress to the elegant wedding ball, the headstrong, willful youngest of Grace and Rainier's children was warned she would be forbidden to attend unless she dressed suitably. Stephanie would not be moved. She stayed away from the ball.

STEPHANIE WEARS A HAND-ME-DOWN

Because her mother hung on to her favorite clothes for years and years, Princess Stephanie benefited from some elegant hand-me-downs. At the Red Cross Ball in 1982 she wore the pale blue faille midcalf strapless dress that Christian Dior had made for Grace in 1956, nearly a decade before Stephanie was born. Despite her normal preference for blue jeans and sportswear, Stephanie seemed to enjoy wearing her mother's clothes. From all reports, Princess Grace got an emotional kick out of seeing her daughter in one of her favorite gowns.

STEPHANIE'S BABY BORN OUT OF WEDLOCK

On May 15, 1992, Princess Stephanie and her former bodyguard, Daniel Ducruet, announced to the media that they were expecting a child and were passionately in love but had no plans to marry. Six months later on November 26, 1992, amidst feverish rumors of wedding plans, Stephanie gave birth to their son out of wedlock in the Princess Grace Hospital in Monte Carlo where her own mother had died a decade earlier. The infant weighed six pounds, eight ounces and was named Louis after his great-great-grandfather, Prince Louis of Monaco. Ducruet was himself born in Monaco in 1964, the son of a French laborer. He joined the Monte Carlo Police Force in 1987 and met Princess Stephanie in 1988 when he was assigned to the palace security staff. Married at the time, he abandoned his wife for a local secretary, Martine Malbouvier, who bore him a son in January, 1992 and then left her to move into Stephanie's Monte Carlo condo.

Throughout Stephanie's pregnancy, she and Daniel posed for photographers in seeming disregard of the feelings of Prince Rainier or Princess Caroline. She has openly flaunted her forty-thousand-dollar-a-month allowance and is said to have bought a New York apartment and a "family-sized" villa in Monaco.

At the time baby Louis was born, Ducruet was facing assault and battery charges in nearby Nice after allegedly beating up a motorist who flashed his high-beam lights at him in traffic. Among Ducruet's interests are a seafood distributing business and such dangerous sports as skydiving. Before learning she was pregnant, Stephanie made several jumps with him. "It was marvelous," she told *People* magazine, while also describing her happiness as being "of such intensity, there are no words to explain it."

STEPHANIE'S PLAYMATE

When Cary Grant's daughter, Jennifer, accompanied him on visits to the south of France, they would often stay with the Rainiers at the palace in Monte Carlo. Because Princess Stephanie and Jennifer were only a year apart in age, they played together during these visits.

STEPHANIE'S ROCK IDOLS

Her all-time favorite, according to rock journalist Henry Edwards, is Tina Turner, who made her "all nervous and emotional" when they met in Monaco. Other rock idols include Dire Straits, R.E.M., and the Scorpions.

FRANCES "FRANCIE" STEVENS

The name of Grace Kelly's character in *To Catch a Thief* was Frances Stevens, known as "Francie." The role was a delicious one. Francie was rich, gorgeous, and bored with visiting Europe's fancier watering holes with her mother in search of thrills and possibly a husband. Although Francie was spoiled rotten and totally self-involved, Grace brought a subtext of yearning to her performance. She enjoyed the pleasures of her life, but in her heart of hearts she knew there was a better way of life with a better quality of man than those usually found at gambling casinos.

Her first reaction to Cary Grant's John Robie was unashamed fascination with his being a jewel thief. This was the adventure she'd been waiting for! In her pursuit of him, she used all of her considerable powers of persuasion. Under director Alfred Hitchcock's tutelage Grace blended aggressive sexuality with sly sophistication in three scenes in particular: when she unexpectedly whirls on Cary Grant and kisses him voluptuously before slamming her door in his face; when she lures him to her suite during an orgasmic fireworks display and tempts him with the jeweled necklace on her otherwise bare chest; and when she "kidnaps" him for a picnic in the country, offering him a leg or a breast to eat. Francie Stevens was utterly captivating. Audiences wanted her to get her man!

STEVENS SCHOOL YEARBOOK PREDICTION

Grace Kelly graduated from the Stevens School in Philadelphia in 1947. Under her senior yearbook photograph was the prediction "She is very likely to become a stage or screen star."

JAMES STEWART

Grace Kelly's costar in *Rear Window*, James Stewart, was captivated by his leading lady but did not become another of her

Grace at her most seductive as Francie Stevens in To Catch a Thief.

older leading man lovers. Instead he and his wife, Gloria, became her devoted friends for the rest of her life. Stewart was among those who participated in Philadelphia's 1982 tribute to her.

Brief Bio: James Maitland Stewart was born May 20, 1908, in Indiana, Pennsylvania, the son of a Scottish hardware store merchant. His primary ambition was to be an engineer but when he failed to make the necessary mathematics grades at Princeton, he joined forces with friends Henry Fonda and Joshua Logan to try his luck at acting on Broadway. In 1934 Stewart's role in the play *Yellow Jack* caught the eye of a Hollywood talent scout. After making more than a dozen forgettable films, he hit his stride with such late 1930s classics as *You Can't Take It with You* and *Mr. Smith Goes to Washington*, and then in 1946 he made *It's a Wonderful Life*, which, ironically, was a box-office flop when first released but has since become enormously popular. He won an Oscar for *The Philadelphia Story* in the role of Mike Connors, which was later played by Frank Sinatra in the 1956 remake, *High Society*, costarring Grace Kelly. Highlights of his fifty-year film career include the Alfred Hitchcock productions *Rear Window* and *Vertigo* as well as *Destry Rides Again*, *Harvey*, *Anatomy of a Murder*, *The Man Who Shot Liberty Valance*, and *Airport*.

During World War II, he attained the highest rank of any show-business figure in the military. Enlisting in the United States Air Force as a private, he soon became a bomber pilot and led more than twenty missions over Germany. By the war's end he was a colonel and by the time he retired from the Air Force Reserve in 1968, he was a brigadier general. He married Gloria McLean in 1949. They have twin daughters, Judy and Kelly. His marriage and family life is known to be one of Hollywood's most successful and loving.

As a TV spokesperson on commercials for Home Cookin', one of Campbell Soup's specialty brands, James Stewart's distinctive and instantly recognizable voice has given him a new

career success in his mid-eighties. What's more, a TV market-
ing firm survey tied him for first place with Bill Cosby as the
celebrity most viewers would trust to sell them something.

*The only leading man who did not fall madly in love with her, a
happily married James Stewart was not totally immune to Grace
Kelly's charms.*

"A SUNNY PLACE FOR SHADY PEOPLE"

W. Somerset Maugham's description of Monaco was "a sunny place for shady people."

A SURPRISE FROM KELL

When Grace Kelly boarded the USS *Constitution* en route to Monaco, she found a surprise awaiting her in her suite. It was a parting gift from her brother, Jack Kelly, Jr. (Kell), a weimaraner dog. Grace's black poodle, Oliver, did not resent the intrusion. The two pets enjoyed the sea voyage enormously.

"A SWEET LITTLE PUSSYCAT"

Princess Stephanie's assessment of her father once his anger has taken its course: "He doesn't stay angry for long. When he starts growling it's best to get out of the way. When he calms down, he's a sweet little pussycat."

"A TATTER'D WEED"

In the fall of 1969 Princess Grace commented on her approaching fortieth birthday (November 12) with a quote from William Shakespeare's Sonnet II:

When forty winters shall besiege thy brow,
And dig deep trenches in thy beauty's field,
Thy youth's proud livery, so gaz'd on now,
Will be a tatter'd weed, of small worth held.

ELIZABETH TAYLOR IN THE PRINCESS GRACE SUITE

In the spring of 1964 Richard Burton appeared on Broadway in *Hamlet*. He and his new wife, Elizabeth Taylor, stayed in the

Princess Grace suite at the Regency Hotel on Park Avenue during the run of the play. The eight-room suite was decorated with eighteenth-century furnishings and cool pastel colors.

A TENTH WEDDING ANNIVERSARY GIFT

In 1966 Prince Rainier asked Grace what she wanted as a tenth wedding anniversary gift.

"A year off" is what she told *Paris Match*.

The gift did not materialize.

"TERRY" KISSES "THE COUNTRY GIRL"

Backstage after the 1955 Academy Awards ceremony, Marlon Brando, holding his Oscar for his best actor role of Terry in *On*

Fellow Oscar winner Marlon Brando congratulates Grace on her award at the 1955 Academy Awards. (UPI/Bettmann)

the Waterfront, playfully kissed best actress Grace Kelly, who was holding tightly to her Oscar for *The Country Girl*.

TIFFANY THE TERRIER

The name of Princess Caroline's miniature Yorkshire terrier in the mid-1970s was Tiffany. The reason for the name? "The best things come from Tiffany's" was Princess Grace's explanation.

TO BE CONTINUED DISCONTINUED

In the spring of 1952, Grace Kelly was cast in her second Broadway play. Titled *To Be Continued*, it opened at the Booth Theater in New York on April 23 and closed the following day.

TOASTED PEANUT BUTTER AND BACON ON SALTINES

As a young woman living alone in her own New York apartment in 1955, Grace Kelly frequently entertained her friends at informal cocktail parties. As an hors d'oeuvre, she often made and served toasted peanut butter and bacon on saltines, a holdover from her teens.

THE "TOO" CATEGORY

Recalling her early auditions, Grace Kelly said people were confused about her "type." Casting directors put her in the "too" category—too tall, too leggy, too skinny being the most common turndowns.

"TOO MUCH SPAGHETTI AND NOODLES!"

Six months into her first pregnancy, Princess Grace had put on twenty-six pounds. With three more months to go before the expected birth, she ruefully attributed her weight gain to "too much spaghetti and noodles!"

THE SPENCER TRACY RUMOR

In her 1985 biography of Katharine Hepburn, *A Remarkable Woman*, Anne Edwards wrote about 1955 rumors of a growing romance between Spencer Tracy and Grace Kelly. She had agreed to costar with him in the film *Tribute to a Bad Man*. According to Edwards, "Tracy claimed the friendship between him and Grace was more business than pleasure, but the fact that Kelly had a penchant for married men did not do a great deal to reassure Kate."

At the time of this whispered-about affair, Tracy and Hepburn had been lovers for more than a decade. They had met in 1941 during the filming of their blockbuster *Woman of the Year*. Though Hepburn gave the impression of relying on him, she was the strong one, and she did not take the rumors about Grace lightly. Tracy was one of America's greatest actors, but he was also a girl chaser whose pursuits included Loretta Young, Joan Crawford, and Kate's close friend Joan Fontaine.

Tribute to a Bad Man is the story of a ruthless horse breeder who is cruel to everyone until love softens him up. Tracy was fifty-five, Grace thirty years younger, a comparable situation to the age difference between her and Gary Cooper in *High Noon*.

After several weeks of meeting with Tracy, Grace finally turned the part down. When the film went into production, Tracy was a week late reporting for work, disappeared for days at a time, and was replaced by James Cagney. Costarring with Greek actress Irene Papas, Cagney received rave reviews for his powerful performance. Presumably the love interest role originally meant for Grace was suitably rewritten for the dark and simmering emotionality of Irene Papas.

There is no record of Kate's reaction to Grace repeating her Tracy Lord role in the *High Society* update of *The Philadelphia Story*. By then, of course, Grace was safely engaged to marry Prince Rainier.

TROUSSEAU FOR A PRINCESS

In the three months between January and April 1956, when she was scheduled to set sail for Monaco and her wedding, Grace

Kelly assembled the trousseau she hoped would meet every possible need in her future life as a princess.

There were custom-made suits and evening gowns from Neiman Marcus in Dallas and a selection of sportswear for every occasion, including a yachting outfit. While on location in Los Angeles for *High Society*, she found time to buy gossamer silk nightgowns and negligees and sets of foundation garments in pink, peach, and black. Returning to New York, she was taken by friends with fashion connections to wholesale houses in the garment district to buy designer clothes at a discount.

Her shoes came from Delman's on Fifth Avenue, her hats from Mr. John, including the white silk jersey turbans that became her headgear of choice on windy days. As if all this weren't sufficient, MGM made her a gift of her entire wardrobe from *High Society*.

"TRUE LOVE" ROYALTIES

"True Love" was a bestselling hit song from the film *High Society*. Although Grace Kelly sang only a few bars with costar Bing Crosby, she received royalties for many years afterward.

MARGARET TRUMAN'S NEIGHBORS WATCH GRACE KELLY GET MARRIED

Townspeople in Independence, Missouri, took time out from preparations for Margaret Truman's April 21, 1956, wedding to watch Grace Kelly's April 19 wedding on television.

THE VERY REVEREND FRANCIS TUCKER

The Delaware-born Catholic priest was Prince Rainier's personal chaplain and devoted friend. It was he who advised the bachelor prince to marry an American, theorizing it would solve two pressing problems. An heir would satisfy the criteria spelled out in Monaco's treaty with France, assuring the principality's independence and its citizens' tax-free status. An

American wife would also attract American press interest in the tiny principality and potentially improve tourism and investment from the United States.

Following his daily routines at Monaco's St. Charles Church, the good-natured blue-eyed priest was amazed and gratified when his rather modest plan turned into the wedding of the century and put Monaco permanently on the map.

Father Tucker worked behind the scenes in making the arrangements for Rainier's December 1955 visit to the United States and the invitation to Philadelphia that resulted in his engagement to Grace Kelly early in the new year.

THE TURNING POINT TURNING POINT

In 1976, 20th Century–Fox was preparing to film *The Turning Point*, the Arthur Laurents script about two middle-aged women who were once ballerinas. Princess Grace was offered her choice of the roles subsequently played by Anne Bancroft and Shirley MacLaine, who both got Academy Award nominations for their performances. After consulting with Prince Rainier, Grace reluctantly turned down the offer. After twenty years of marriage, this was the final turning point in her realization that she would never make another feature film.

TWENTY-SIX YEARS AND SIX MONTHS

Princess Grace lived the first twenty-six-and-a-half years of her life in America as Grace Kelly—and the last twenty-six-and-a-half years as Monaco's reigning consort.

THE TWO CAROLINES

In the mid-1970s Princess Caroline and Caroline Kennedy were the world's two most famous teenagers. While "Jackie" followers lay in ambush wherever the widowed Mrs. Onassis and her daughter might be, the European press "discovered" Princess Grace's beautiful, provocative first born. Princess Caroline reached international status when *Time* magazine commissioned Norman Parkinson to photograph her for its cover wearing French couturier clothes and with her hair styled by her mother's old friend, Alexandre.

UNCOMFORTABLE FATHER-IN-LAW

Grace Kelly's father was extremely uncomfortable staying in his new son-in-law's Monaco palace. According to his nephew, Charles V. Kelly, Jr., Jack Kelly considered life with the Grimaldis "pretentious." He hated having servants offering to cater to his every whim. To have privacy, his way of dismissing them was to wave them away and bark, "I'll call you when I need you."

UNDER AN ASSUMED NAME

Following the announcement of his engagement to Grace Kelly, Prince Rainier traveled to Los Angeles in February 1956 to visit his future wife while she was filming *High Society.* He had thought that after the initial furor, the press would leave them alone. He was wrong. He and Grace were besieged wherever they went. The unwanted attention was beginning to get on his nerves. When it was time to leave on his return trip to Monaco, he thought he could fool the press by booking his air flight under the assumed name C. Monte. He was wrong again! The press came out in force to wish him *"bon voyage."*

UNE BONNE FOURCHETTE

An admiring French expression for a woman with a good appetite and an appreciation of food is *une bonne fourchette.* The phrase was often affectionately applied to Princess Grace.

UNFULFILLED PLANS

In the months before she died, Princess Grace was involved in the development of several projects. Among them were a film about Raoul Wallenberg, the Swedish diplomat who saved thousands of Jews from being shipped to concentration camps during World War II and was then himself interred by the Russians, his fate a mystery to this day. Also on the drawing board was a film based on a Gore Vidal short story, "The Dangerous Gift."

AN UNHAPPY PRINCESS ON A TRIP TO THAILAND

Just five months before her death, Princess Grace and Prince Rainier visited Bangkok, Thailand. Press photographs reveal a sadly overweight and puffy woman wearing a striped outfit that only exaggerated her heft and a white turban that served to show how her once-perfect face had changed as well. Prince Rainier's grumpy appearance in the Bangkok photographs seems to substantiate rumors about "the battling Grimaldis."

UPSTAGED BY JACKIE

At the International Red Cross Ball in Seville, Spain, in 1967, the press virtually ignored Princess Grace and Prince Rainier in favor of Jacqueline Kennedy, prompting the outraged princess to disappear into the powder room and stay there fuming for an hour. A few days later Jackie again stole the limelight at the bullring, when Spain's leading toreros, El Cordobes, Paco Camino, and El Viti, offered their hats and first bulls to the former first lady instead of Grace.

EDITH VAN CLEVE

The MCA talent agent who handled both Grace Kelly and Marlon Brando early in their careers was Edith Van Cleve. Later both would be represented by Jay Kanter of the same agency.

VARIETY ANNOUNCES THE MARRIAGE

True to its standardized formula for covering entertainment world births, deaths, and marriages, the show business newspaper *Variety* announced simply, *"Marriages*—Grace Kelly to Prince Rainier III. Bride is film star; groom is non-pro."

THE VATICAN ANNULS CAROLINE'S FIRST MARRIAGE

In July 1992 after a ten-year examination, the Vatican announced the annulment of the marriage of Princess Caroline and her first husband, Philippe Junot. The couple was married on June 29, 1978, and divorced on October 9, 1980. Caroline immediately petitioned for an annulment in order to get on with her life. While waiting for a decision, she married Stefano Casiraghi in a civil ceremony in 1983 and bore him three children. Her continuing efforts to attain an annulment and marry Casiraghi in church were tragically nullified by his death in a 1990 speedboat accident. As for their three children, Archbishop Joseph Sardou of Monaco has said, "Unfortunately, since Stefano is dead and she has no possibility of marrying him, the children remain illegitimate in the eyes of the church."

On a happier note, the annulment cleared the way for Caroline to marry French film star Vincent Lindon in church.

A VERY GOOD YEAR FOR GRACE'S CHILDREN

Looking back, 1972 was perhaps the happiest and most contented year of Princess Grace's married life. Her children were healthy, intelligent, and well behaved. Caroline, fifteen, Albert, fourteen, and Stephanie, seven, were a source of tremendous maternal pride. In a letter to an American friend Grace called them her jewels, "wonderful, sweet and adorable." Caroline was still a schoolgirl at a convent in England and impressed her mother as being "much more sensible than I was at her age." Albert struck his mother as being "quiet but strong, a dreamer who possesses a sweet nature." As for Stephanie, Grace characterized her youngest child as a "seven-year-old teenager" with an irresistible charm that she used to twist people around her little finger.

THE VILLA IBERIA (SPANISH VILLA)

This was the name of Prince Rainier's bachelor hideaway at Cap Ferrat a few miles west of Monaco on the French Riviera. It was where he had lived for six years with actress Gisele Pascal and where he spent his last night alone as a bachelor before his wedding day.

Until his marriage he had treated his palace as a place of business, where he conducted the affairs of state, rather than as a home. After his marriage he and Grace made the palace their home. The Villa Iberia was sold shortly thereafter.

VINTAGE CARS

Prince Rainier's vintage car collection includes a 1903 De Dion Bouton and a 1938 Packard eight-cylinder. All told he owns nearly fifty old cars and plans to house them in a Monte Carlo museum for the pleasure of tourists.

"WAIT SIX MONTHS, OLEG!"

At their very first meeting Grace's mother told Oleg Cassini in no uncertain terms that he was not good marriage material so far as the Kelly family were concerned. He was divorced, he had a checkered past, and he was a playboy.

There were religious considerations that could not be ignored, Margaret Kelly explained. Grace was deeply committed to her Catholic faith; love alone would not be enough to sustain a marriage.

With Grace sitting in silence beside her, Margaret Kelly concluded the "interview" with Cassini by demanding a six-month moratorium on wedding plans. Although Grace talked about defying her family, even suggesting she and Oleg elope, no definite plans were made. The romance lasted for nearly two years and on Oleg's part was still heading toward marriage when Grace broke the news about her decision to marry Prince Rainier.

WARTIME "SERVICE"

When the United States entered World War II in 1941, Grace Kelly was twelve years old. Along with other young girls in the Philadelphia area, she became a "Pink Girl" hospital volunteer in 1942. Her job was to carry food trays to patients. According to journalist Patty de Roulf in *Motion Picture* magazine in 1955, "On one occasion she brought a tray to a man whose eyes were bandaged. Grace not only offered to feed him but decided to add zest to the repast." As she spooned out a thin tasteless broth, she crooned, "You are now tasting rare green turtle soup, imported directly from the king's palace in Barcelona!" A lowly veal chop was described by Grace in equally glowing terms, and when it came to dessert, Grace enthused, "And now, two waiters are lighting the brandy on your crepes suzettes. My how the flame glows! Now they are dipping them out of the gleaming chafing dish. Gee, it smells divine!"

Thus, de Roulf was told, "She made tapioca pudding sound wonderful."

MARY WAYTE—IS SHE WAITING FOR ALBERT?

Prince Albert's long-term friendship with U.S. swimming champion Mary Wayte has been rumored to be on the brink of matrimony since they met in 1985.

Mary won a gold medal for the two-hundred-meter free-style in the 1984 Olympics in Los Angeles and signed with NBC as a swimming analyst during the 1992 summer Olympics. In March 1992 she was with Albert in France for the winter Olympics at Albertville and watched nervously as Albert, captain of the Monaco Olympic bobsled team, risked his neck hurtling down the treacherous, winding bobsled run at over seventy miles per hour.

Following the 1990 death of Princess Caroline's husband, Stefano, in a high-speed sports event, nobody in Albert's family could bear to go to the bobsled run in La Plagne in the French Alps to watch him compete.

According to one report, Mary waited near the arrival point for the Monaco bobsled to appear. Even though he came in a miserable forty-third in the two-man bobsled race and a disappointing twenty-third in the four-man, Mary hugged him and said he had done great. *Time* magazine did not agree. In a review of the 1992 Winter Olympics it cited Albert as "worst dilettante, royal division."

Friends who are urging the Monaco heir apparent to marry are quick to point out Mary Wayte's credentials. She's American like Albert's mother, she speaks French, she loves sports, and she prefers living in Europe—all adding up to the makings of a potential new American princess for the Grimaldis.

THE WEDDING ATTENDANTS: HERS

Grace Kelly was attended by her older sister, Peggy Kelly Davis, as matron of honor; bridesmaids Judith Kanter, Rita Gam, Maree Pamp, Carolyn Reybold, Sally Parrish Richardson, and Bettina Gray; and six children, including Peggy's two daughters, Meg and Mary Lee, as flower girls.

THE WEDDING ATTENDANTS: HIS

Prince Rainier was attended by three best men, his cousin, Count Charles de Polignac; his friend and house governor, Lieutenant Colonel Jean-Marie Ardant, and his soon-to-be brother-in-law, Grace Kelly's brother, Kell.

THE WEDDING CAKE

Grace and Rainier's wedding cake weighed two-hundred pounds, consisted of seven layers, and was decorated with the Grimaldi coat of arms, cupids, and confectionary models of the palace. It was topped by a scarlet-and-gold crown.

THE WEDDING DRESS

A gift to Grace from MGM, the wedding dress was a spectacular vision of exquisite loveliness. Created by her good friend Helen Rose, MGM's Academy Award–winning chief costume designer, it was in every sense a labor of love. The most expensive dress Helen Rose ever made, it featured 125-year-old rose point lace bought from a museum. Three dozen seamstresses worked under Rose's supervision on twenty-five yards of silk taffeta, one-hundred yards of silk net, and three-hundred yards of Valenciennes lace for petticoats alone.

The train was three-and-a-half yards long. The long-sleeved rose point lace bodice was reembroidered to hide the seams. The gown fastened down the front with tiny lace buttons and fit over a silk flesh-toned underbodice.

The overskirt was bell-shaped, the fullness in back laid in pleats at the waist and flaring into a fan shape at the bottom. The underskirt was in fact three petticoats in crepe and taffeta.

The bridal veil, embroidered with rose point lace and covered with several thousand tiny seed pearls, was designed to frame Grace's face. Her Juliet cap was made of matching lace with a wreath of small orange blossoms and leaves fashioned from seed pearls. Appliquéd on the back of the veil were two miniature lace lovebirds. Fashion critics hailed Helen Rose's creation as a masterwork not only for its intrinsic beauty and elegance but also because it enhanced its wearer's slender, dignified beauty on the most solemn occasion of her life. To complete the picture as she walked down the aisle of the Cathedral of St. Nicholas on her father's arm, the bride carried a prayer book covered in the same taffeta as was used in her wedding dress, the cross on the book embroidered in pearls.

WEDDING GIFTS

Among Grace and Rainier's wedding gifts were

- An antique writing desk from the Cary Grants
- A diamond and ruby necklace from the Société des Bains de Mer (the SBM syndicate in Monaco)
- A Rolls-Royce from the citizens of Monaco
- A Cinemascope screen and two thirty-five millimeter projectors to equip a private screening room in the palace so that Grace especially could see American films from a group of friends from Philadelphia
- A gold picture frame from Americans living in Monaco
- A porcelain table service from Germans living in Monaco
- A matching pair of decorated helmsman wheels for the royal yacht from the government of France
- A tiara and diamond and ruby bracelet for Princess Grace from Aristotle Onassis plus a donation of a million francs to the Monaco Red Cross
- A table lamp from Prince Rainier's cousin, the marquis de Polignac
- A china coffee service from President Gronchi of Italy
- A silver panther from the palace staff
- A crystal decanter and ship's barometer from President Coty of France
- An underwater skin-diving camera from Monaco's utilities company
- Bonbon dishes from Princess Serge Wolkonsky
- Twin pitchers from the mayor of Nice
- A two-foot-square glass treasure chest containing an assortment of gold pins, bracelets, pens, pencils, and a small diamond-studded jewelry case from the Aga Khan
- A bone and gold hatchet from the Speleological Club of Monaco

WEDDING GIFTS: GRACE TO RAINIER

Among the gifts Grace Kelly brought to Monaco for her soon-to-be husband was a gold cigarette case studded with jewels.

WEDDING GIFTS: RAINIER TO GRACE

Among Prince Rainier's gifts to his new wife were a pearl necklace and a diamond-studded bracelet.

THE WEDDING: GRACE AND RAINIER EXCHANGE VOWS

At the point in the elaborate religious ceremony where the bride and groom exchange vows, Monaco's bishop, Monsignor Gilles Barthe, asked, "Rainier Louis Henri Maxence Bertrand, will you take Grace Patricia here present for your lawful wife, according to the rite of our Holy Mother Church?"

"Yes, I will." (*Oui, je veux.*)

Turning to the bride, "Grace Patricia, will you take Rainier Louis Henri Maxence Bertrand for your lawful husband, according to the rite of our Holy Mother the Church?"

"Yes, I will." (*Oui, je veux.*)

Satisfied with their replies, the bishop then said, "I declare you united in marriage in the name of the Father, the Son, and the Holy Ghost."

"THE WEDDING OF THE CENTURY"

That's what the world media called the 1956 wedding of Grace Kelly and Prince Rainier.

The same tag was given to the 1981 wedding uniting Lady Diana Spencer and Prince Charles.

THE WEDDING: PICKPOCKETS

Professional pickpockets from all over Europe descended on Monaco for what seemed to be "easy pickings" among the vast

A thoughtful portrait of Grace Kelly taken during the hectic days before her wedding, early 1956.

crowds attending public and private events as part of the wedding festivities.

Visitors and guests were warned to beware of jostling and to watch their valuables. Although there were some unpleasant incidents, the Monaco security force rounded up a large number of pickpockets and marched them handcuffed through the streets of Monte Carlo to custody.

THE WEDDING SCRAPBOOK

Following her 1956 wedding, Princess Grace asked a palace aide to collect the mountain of newspaper and magazine clippings in a scrapbook along with photographs and other mementos of the weeklong festivities. Later she admitted that she let more than a year go by before she could bring herself to look at the scrapbook.

THE WEDDING: THE CIVIL CEREMONY

April 18, 1956, in the palace throne room. Grace Kelly wore a pale pink gown and carried a bridal bouquet; Prince Rainier wore a black morning suit with gray striped trousers. The room was hot because of the powerful lights needed for the television cameras and also for the MGM crew filming for an eventual documentary. The bride and groom sat on matching red velvet chairs a few feet apart. The ceremony, conducted in French, took forty minutes to legally unite Grace and Rainier as man and wife.

WEDDING TRIVIA

• Aristotle Onassis ordered hundreds of carnations to be dropped by plane on Prince Rainier's 138-foot yacht, the *Deo Juvante II*, but most of the flowers missed the target and landed elsewhere.
• During the Nuptial Mass at the Cathedral of St. Nicholas, two men dressed as priests were arrested as pickpockets.
• At the wedding reception a scuffle broke out in the orchestra when an Italian photographer was discovered in the bassoon section taking pictures.
• More than two thousand reporters and photographers covered the wedding, twice the press coverage of the Normandy invasion twelve years earlier in 1944.
• During the wedding rehearsal, Prince Rainier bit his fingernails.
• The religious ceremony was seen live on television by thirty million people in nine European countries and hours later by untold millions throughout the world.
• Unlike all other marriages in Monaco, no banns were posted for Rainier and Grace, the theory being that that way nobody could object to it.

THE WEDDING: WHICH PAPER DO YOU READ?

If Americans reading about the Monaco wedding read more than one newspaper, they were in for confusion. The press differed in what it saw and heard. The palace throne room was described by the INS news service as being decorated in gilded damask, while the *Herald Tribune* thought it was crimson damask and the *New York Post* declared it tapestried and frescoed.

According to the United Press International, the bride had tears in her eyes, while the Associated Press insisted, "No tears." And when it came to her saying yes, she would marry him, to the bishop of Monaco, some reporters in the cathedral "heard" her say *"Je veux"* (I will), while others heard only a succinct *"Oui."*

Four months after the wedding the *New York Daily Mirror*, a usually hard-hitting tabloid, turned all gooey and whimsical in reporting the announcement of an expected Grimaldi heir. Under a photograph of Princess Grace and Prince Rainier, the caption said: "Monaco weather forecast a little Rainier in February."

THE WEDDING(S): COMPARISONS BETWEEN GRACE AND MARGARET

Grace Kelly and Margaret Truman got married six thousand miles and two days apart. Some comparisons between the two weddings:

Grace	Margaret
Monaco's population was twenty-three thousand.	The population of Independence, Missouri, was fifty thousand.
Her religious ceremony was at the Cathedral of St. Nicholas.	Her religious ceremony was at Trinity Episcopal Church.
Her matron of honor was her sister Peggy Kelly Davis.	Her matron of honor was Drucie Snyder Horton.
The religious wedding ceremony was conducted by Bishop Gilles Barthe.	The religious ceremony was conducted by the Reverend Patric Hutton.
It took one hour.	It took twelve minutes.

Her wedding gown was created by top Hollywood designer Helen Rose, who attended the wedding.

Her wedding gown was created by Italian designer Fontana, who traveled from Rome to attend the wedding.

The lace on Grace's gown was 125-year-old rose point purchased from a museum.

The lace and veil of Margaret's gown were two-hundred-year-old Venetian heirloom.

Grace's prayer book was covered with the same taffeta as used in her wedding gown, its cross embroidered in pearls.

Margaret's prayer book and purse were covered with gold lace and topped with white camellias and stephanotis.

Grace and Rainier's honeymoon trip was a monthlong Mediterranean cruise on their yacht, the *Deo Juvante II*.

Margaret and Clifton's honeymoon destination was a secret hideaway in the Bahamas.

Grace's married name became Her Serene Highness Princess Grace Patricia.

Margaret's married name became Mrs. E. Clifton Daniel in private life and remained Margaret Truman professionally.

WELCOME GUESTS AT OTHER ROYAL WEDDINGS

Although the royal families of Europe and Great Britain had snubbed Grace and Rainier's wedding, sending gifts and representatives instead of attending in person, attitudes gradually changed due to the growing popularity of the Monégasque sovereigns. In due course their Serene Highnesses were invited to the royal weddings of King Constantine II of Greece to Princess Anne-Marie of Denmark in Athens in 1964, of Britain's Princess Anne to Captain Mark Phillips in 1973, and of Prince Charles to Lady Diana Spencer in the summer of 1981.

MARGOT WENDICE

The name of Grace Kelly's character in *Dial M for Murder* was
Margot Wendice. Married to over-the-hill tennis champion

*Ray Milland as Grace Kelly's husband pretending to play the good host
to visitor Robert Cummings as he plans to involve Cummings in his
plot to murder Grace in* Dial M for Murder.

Tony Wendice, played by Ray Milland, she has fallen in love with an American mystery writer played by Robert Cummings. Margot is the one with the money. When Tony discovers her infidelity, he realizes she may divorce him and leave him penniless. That's when he blackmails a former schoolmate into murdering her.

Tony's plan is a masterpiece of suspense. He is out with friends. Margot has retired early. The would-be killer is in the Wendice flat when Tony's phone call lures Margot to the desk where the killer is waiting to pounce. While Tony listens coldly, Margot struggles with her attacker and stabs him with scissors she was ironically using to assemble Tony's press clippings in a scrapbook!

When she sobs hysterically into the phone, begging her husband to help her, the ever-resourceful Tony twists things around to make it seem that the victim was actually blackmailing his wife and that she killed him after a violent quarrel. Charged with murder and condemned to death, Margot never suspects her husband's betrayal until the mystery writer and the police inspector played by John Williams uncover the truth with literally hours to spare before her scheduled execution.

Margot Wendice was the first of three roles Grace Kelly played for director Alfred Hitchcock. The pivotal scene was Margot's life-and-death struggle with her attacker. She was the vulnerable woman in a flimsy nightgown, aroused from sleep and talking to her husband, the essence of safety and security, when suddenly she must fight like a tiger for her life. Although the struggle takes less than two minutes on screen, Hitchcock spent a week filming what is considered one of his most heart-stopping scenes.

WHAT IF GRACE HAD TWINS?

Halfway through her first pregnancy, Princess Grace visited New York with her husband. A reporter looking for something different asked what would happen if she had twins. Who would be the heir apparent? Prince Rainier replied calmly, "The first to be born, regardless of sex."

WHAT LOVERS DID GRACE "SHARE" WITH MARILYN MONROE?

Oleg Cassini, Clark Gable, and Frank Sinatra were all at one time lovers of both Marilyn Monroe and Grace Kelly.

WHAT "MA" KELLY NEVER KNEW . . .

In 1975, shortly after threatening to go to the media and denounce her son Kell's friendship with transsexual Rachel Harlow, Margaret Kelly suffered a severe stroke. Her vicious attack on her only son effectively destroyed his hopes for a political career and undermined whatever self-confidence he may have achieved after the death of his father.

"Ma" Kelly lapsed into a near-vegetative state, where she remained for nearly fifteen years. She died in January 1990 at the age of ninety-one, never knowing that Grace had died in 1982, Kell had suffered a fatal heart attack while jogging in Philadelphia in 1984, and Princess Caroline had borne three royal grandchildren she would never see.

WHEN DID RAINIER PROPOSE?

The official version is New Year's Eve, 1955. To close friends, Rainier revealed it was a few days earlier but during Christmas week, adding that he asked her quite simply, "Will you marry me?"

To which she replied with equal simplicity, "Yes."

WHY GRACE HATED HOLLYWOOD

Interviewed in 1954, Grace Kelly explained her hatred of life in Hollywood: "Fear covers everything out here like the smog."

WHY MARRY A MAN SHE BARELY KNEW?

According to top celebrity biographer James Spada, "When Grace met Prince Rainier, she was ready and eager to make a drastic change in her life. She was deeply disappointed in Hollywood, wounded by the salacious publicity her romantic liaisons had engendered, and afraid that she had achieved all she could professionally, that her career could do nothing but wane." Moreover, Spada makes clear that she wanted to be married and have children. Bred into her from childhood was the tenet "A woman's greatest achievement is being a wife and mother."

"A WILD TEENAGER"

In 1983, a year after Princess Grace's death, *People* magazine ran an in-depth retrospective. The article quotes an early Philadelphia acquaintance who even after four decades preferred anonymity: "Grace was a wild teenager, but everyone hides it. She gets loyalty from everybody, but those of us who knew her remember her."

WILL RAINIER ABDICATE IN 1997?

Monaco insiders point to the fact that January 8, 1997, marks the seven-hundredth anniversary of the principality. All things being equal, the seventy-five-year-old ruler might well choose that historic date to abdicate in favor of his son, Prince Albert, who would then be forty, mature and experienced enough to take his country into its eighth century.

"A WOMAN HAS TO GIVE MORE"

On the twentieth anniversary of her marriage to Prince Rainier, Princess Grace attributed its success to her conviction that "marriage is a partnership but not an equal one. A woman has to give more."

"WORDS UPON THE WIND"

The song Princess Stephanie wrote in 1985 and dedicated to her mother's memory was "Words upon the Wind." She recorded it for Epic/WTG on an LP called *Stephanie*, which was produced by her former lover Ron Bloom. Most poignant of her lyrics are the lines "I'll see you again, Mother/until then/It's words upon the wind."

"THE WORLD'S FIRST INDOOR COUNTRY?"

On a visit to Houston, Texas, Prince Rainier was overwhelmed by the Astrodome and its nine-acre climate-controlled seating. Asked how he would like to have a similar dome for Monaco, he quipped, "We could be the world's first indoor country."

THE WORLD'S LONGEST-SERVING RULER

As the thirty-third prince of Monaco, Rainier III not only represents the oldest ruling family in Europe but since the 1989 death of Japan's Emperor Hirohito, he has become the world's longest-serving ruler. He ascended the throne of Monaco in May 1949 at the age of twenty-six.

"WOULD YOU LIKE A LEG OR A BREAST?"

One of Grace Kelly's most-quoted movie lines was "Would you like a leg or a breast?" It's what she flirtatiously asks Cary Grant when offering him some cold chicken during a seductive picnic scene in *To Catch a Thief*. The sassiness of this dialogue may seem quaint to 1990s filmgoers. It should, however, be enjoyed within the context of the prim sexuality of 1950s films. In contrast to today's explicit eroticism, Kelly's brazen pursuit of Grant throughout the film generated its own kind of heat.

SAM ZIMBALIST

Movie producer Sam Zimbalist saw Grace Kelly's screen test for Gregory Ratoff's *Taxi* and was so impressed by her that he and director John Ford cast her as the inhibited Linda who falls passionately in love with Clark Gable in *Mogambo*.

FRED ZINNEMANN

Born in Vienna on April 29, 1907, the Academy Award–winning director immigrated to America in 1929, bent on a film career. Inspired by such European film pioneers as Eric von Stroheim and King Vidor, he headed straight for Hollywood. All he could get was an extra's part in *All Quiet on the Western Front*. By 1952, when he cast Grace Kelly as the inhibited Quaker bride of Sheriff Kane in *High Noon*, Zinnemann had assisted Busby Berkeley in 1930s musicals, directed Pete Smith comedy shorts for MGM, and directed his first feature film, *The Search* (1948), starring Montgomery Clift.

Directing *High Noon* catapulted him into the superdirector category, earning him subsequent Oscars for *From Here to Eternity* (1953) and *A Man for All Seasons* (1966) and audience acclaim for the terrifying *The Day of the Jackal* (1973) and *Julia* (1977).

Some stories about Grace Kelly and her white gloves may be apocryphal, but Zinnemann himself confirmed the truth about his first meeting with Grace Kelly in 1952. Sent by her agent, Jay Kanter, to the studio to meet Zinnemann, she did wear a ladylike outfit and ladylike white gloves.

"It wasn't so much the gloves," Zinnemann later told an interviewer. "It was the personality and manner to go with them." Most actresses were uninhibited. The quality he wanted for Amy Kane, Gary Cooper's young wife, was straitlaced, virginal inhibition.

While filming *High Noon*, Grace Kelly conducted a very passionate and very public love affair with the fifty-one-year-old Gary Cooper. From all reports, Zinnemann was also smitten by the newcomer but was content to express his affection with loving close-ups that made more of her relatively small role than was necessary—infuriating Mexican actress Katy Jurado, who played Will Kane's mistress in the film.

Grace expressed her appreciation with the courteous formality one might expect: As she said in *Motion Picture* magazine, "I'll never be able to thank Fred Zinnemann for what he did for me. He and Mr. [Stanley] Kramer were the ones who proved to me that moviemaking is as great a creative art as the stage, and that those who talk down the movies just haven't seen or been in the right pictures."

High Noon earned Gary Cooper a best actor Oscar. Ironically, director John Ford didn't care too much for Grace's performance in *High Noon*. But he had seen her screen test for *Taxi*, a role she didn't get, which prompted him to test her for *Mogambo*, a role she did get—along with Clark Gable, if only temporarily.

MAURICE ZOLOTOW

One of America's most respected biographers of entertainment personalities ranging from the Lunts to John Wayne and author of perhaps the best book about Marilyn Monroe, Maurice Zolotow was perplexed by the insatiable public hunger for articles, books, and news coverage of Grace Kelly and her life as Princess Grace of Monaco.

In an article about her in 1961, five years after her marriage, he wrote, "One of the curious questions of modern public opinion is why the world's imagination continues to be intrigued by a certain tall, slender, thirty-two-year-old blonde, who is married, has two children, is nearsighted, plays the piano, loves dogs, hot jazz, and practical jokes, hates the sun and crowds and small talk, adores rainstorms and long solitary walks and serious novels, and has for six years contributed absolutely nothing of any world-shaking social, artistic, political, or economic importance that would justify the amount of attention she gets."

CONTENTS